INTRODUCTION

CHAPTER 1: UNDERSTANDING POST-POSTMODERNISM

CHAPTER 2: EMPHASIS ON NETWORKS AND RELATIONSHIPS

CHAPTER 3: ETHICAL CONSIDERATIONS IN LEADERSHIP

CHAPTER 4: NEW FORMS OF POWER AND RESISTANCE

CHAPTER 5: THE INTEGRATION OF PLAY AND CREATIVITY

CHAPTER 6: HYBRID APPROACHES IN ORGANIZATIONAL THEORY

CHAPTER 7: ADAPTING TO THE GLOBAL LANDSCAPE

APPENDICES

Thank you for picking up my book. Your support means a lot, and I hope you find the read both enjoyable and insightful. Beyond being an author, my work extends into research and consultancy within organizational behavior and leadership. I engage with a broad spectrum of clients, from individuals to larger teams and organizations, offering guidance in leadership development.

For a deeper dive into my professional background and consulting philosophy, several websites are available. There, you'll also find my contact details. I'm eager to hear your thoughts on the book or discuss potential collaboration in leadership coaching.

Discover more about my work and other publications related to leadership and organizational behavior at my personal website, https://thomaspatrickhuber.com.

Learn about my specific approach to leadership coaching and consulting at https://elevateus.ch, the official website of my company.

Lastly, in case you want to reach out to me directly please send me an email at thomaspatrick@mac.com.

I appreciate your support in purchasing this book and look forward to connecting with you.

Wishing you an enlightening journey,

Thomas P Huber, PhD, MS ECS

Introduction

In our ever changing and rapid evolving landscape of contemporary business, traditional leadership paradigms often fall short. Enter post-postmodernism, also known as metamodernism, a forward-thinking approach that offers fresh, pragmatic strategies for today's leaders. This book delves into how metamodernism can reshape leadership, providing practical, adaptable frameworks that address the complexities of modern organizations.

Metamodernism transcends the skepticism of postmodernism, offering constructive solutions that acknowledge the intricacies of contemporary business environments. Leaders are equipped with tools to manage complexity effectively, driving their organizations toward practical and achievable goals.

When corporate social responsibility and sustainability are paramount, ethical leadership is more critical than ever. Metamodernism emphasizes integrating ethical considerations into all aspects of leadership, meeting the rising expectations of stakeholders and ensuring long-term organizational success. The fast-paced nature of today's business world demands leaders who can adapt quickly to change. Metamodernism advocates for flexibility and responsiveness, encouraging leaders to embrace uncertainty and navigate complex scenarios with confidence.

Gone are the days of rigid, top-down leadership structures. Modern organizations thrive on collaboration and networked approaches. This book explores how distributed leadership can enhance innovation and responsiveness, reflecting the interconnected reality of today's business landscape.

Technology is a driving force in shaping modern organizational structures and processes. Leaders must leverage digital tools to stay competitive. Metamodern strategies incorporate technological integration, providing insights on how to utilize digital advancements for effective management.

Globalization has made cultural understanding a crucial aspect of leadership. Metamodernism highlights the importance of navigating diverse cultural perspectives, enabling leaders to manage international teams effectively and engage with global markets. Employee engagement and empowerment are vital for fostering creativity and innovation. Metamodern leadership prioritizes creating environments where employees feel valued and motivated, driving individual and organizational growth.

Every business scenario is unique, and a one-size-fits-all approach doesn't suffice. Metamodernism encourages balancing insights from both modernist and postmodernist perspectives, allowing leaders to apply the most effective strategies for each situation.

This book is your guide to understanding and implementing metamodern leadership principles. By embracing these forward-thinking strategies, you can lead your organization through the complexities of the modern business environment with agility, ethical integrity, and innovative spirit.

Three terms have emerged as pivotal in understanding and navigating contemporary challenges: post-postmodernism, metamodernism, and digimodernism. Each represents a shift from the paradigms of the past, offering nuanced perspectives and practical frameworks suited to today's complex business environments.

Post-Postmodernism

Post-postmodernism is a reaction to and evolution beyond postmodernism. While postmodernism was characterized by skepticism, deconstruction, and a focus on the relative and subjective nature of reality, post-postmodernism seeks to build constructively on these insights. It acknowledges the fragmented and fluid nature of contemporary life but strives for coherence and practical solutions. In business, post-postmodernism encourages leaders to embrace complexity and ambiguity, moving beyond mere critique to develop actionable strategies that address the dynamic realities of modern organizations.

Metamodernism

Metamodernism occupies a middle ground between modernist optimism and postmodernist skepticism. It is characterized by a dynamic interplay between these opposing sensibilities, oscillating between hope and doubt, sincerity and irony, and order and chaos. This framework is particularly relevant for business leaders who must navigate a world that is simultaneously interconnected and unpredictable. Metamodernism promotes a leadership style that is adaptable, ethically grounded, and capable of synthesizing diverse perspectives to find innovative solutions. Leaders are encouraged to be pragmatic yet visionary, blending practical management with creative and forward-thinking approaches.

Digimodernism

Digimodernism focuses on the impact of digital technology on culture, society, and organizational structures. It recognizes that digital advancements have fundamentally altered how we communicate, work, and organize. Digimodernism emphasizes the need for leaders to understand and leverage digital tools to drive innovation and efficiency. This perspective highlights the importance of digital literacy, the integration of technology into all aspects of business operations, and the potential for technology to disrupt traditional models. Leaders must be adept at navigating the digital landscape, using data and technology to inform decision-making and create agile, responsive organizations. Below are key themes that we will explore in greater detail in the book;

Complexity and Adaptability

All three paradigms emphasize the importance of embracing complexity and remaining adaptable. Whether through the constructive pragmatism of post-postmodernism, the oscillating sensibilities of metamodernism, or the technological focus of digimodernism, leaders are encouraged to be flexible and responsive to change.

Ethical and Responsible Leadership

Ethical considerations are central to these contemporary frameworks. In a world where corporate social responsibility and sustainability are increasingly important, leaders must integrate ethical principles into their strategies and practices. This involves not only adhering to ethical standards but also fostering a culture of integrity and accountability within their organizations.

Collaboration and Networking

The traditional top-down leadership model is being replaced by more collaborative and networked approaches. These paradigms recognize the value of relationships, connectivity, and distributed leadership. By fostering collaboration and leveraging the strengths of diverse teams, leaders can drive innovation and resilience.

Technological Integration

Understanding and leveraging technology is a key theme, especially in digimodernism. Leaders must be proficient in digital tools and strategies, using technology to enhance productivity, innovation, and competitive advantage. This involves staying current with technological trends and integrating digital solutions into all facets of the organization.

Post-postmodernism, metamodernism, and digimodernism provide valuable frameworks for contemporary business leadership. By understanding and applying the principles of these paradigms, leaders can navigate the complexities of the modern business environment with agility, ethical integrity, and a forward-thinking approach. This book aims to equip you with the knowledge and tools needed to lead effectively in a rapidly changing world.

In the face of unprecedented changes and challenges in the business world, traditional leadership models are increasingly inadequate. The rapid pace of technological advancements, shifting societal expectations, and the complexities of global interconnectedness demand a fresh approach to leadership. Contemporary businesses require leaders who can navigate ambiguity, foster innovation, and maintain ethical integrity in an ever-changing landscape.

Post-postmodernism, metamodernism, and digimodernism emerge as timely responses to these needs, each offering distinct yet complementary frameworks that move beyond outdated paradigms. These new perspectives encourage leaders to adopt a more fluid and responsive mindset, capable of adapting to the unpredictable nature of the modern business environment. By focusing on holistic and integrative approaches, these frameworks enable leaders to address multifaceted challenges with creativity and agility.

In post-postmodernism, there is a call for leaders to move beyond mere critique and deconstruction, emphasizing instead the creation of actionable and practical solutions. This approach values the complexity of real-world problems and seeks to develop strategies that are both innovative and grounded in reality. Leaders are encouraged to foster environments where diverse ideas can flourish, leading to more robust and resilient organizations.

Metamodernism, with its emphasis on oscillation between modernist certainty and postmodernist doubt, advocates for a leadership style that embraces both hope and skepticism. This duality allows leaders to remain optimistic about the future while being realistic about the present challenges. By balancing these perspectives, leaders can inspire their teams with a vision of what is possible while remaining grounded in practical realities.

Digimodernism places a strong emphasis on the transformative power of digital technology. In an era where digital tools and platforms are reshaping every aspect of business, leaders must be adept at leveraging these technologies to drive growth and innovation. This includes not only understanding the latest technological trends but also creating a culture that embraces digital transformation and continuous learning.

Ethical leadership is a cornerstone of these new paradigms, reflecting a broader societal shift towards greater accountability and transparency. Leaders are expected to go beyond profit-driven motives, considering the broader impact of their decisions on society and the environment. This holistic view of business success encompasses sustainability, social responsibility, and the well-being of all stakeholders.

The shift towards more collaborative and distributed leadership models also reflects the interconnected nature of contemporary organizations. In a world where hierarchies are flattening and networks are becoming more prominent, leaders must be skilled in facilitating collaboration and harnessing the collective intelligence of their teams. This involves creating inclusive environments where every team member feels valued and empowered to contribute.

Cultural sensitivity is increasingly important in today's globalized business environment. Leaders must navigate diverse cultural contexts with empathy and understanding, building bridges across differences to foster a cohesive and inclusive organizational culture. This cultural agility enables businesses to thrive in international markets and build strong, diverse teams.

Empowering employees to take initiative and innovate is another key aspect of modern leadership. By creating supportive environments that encourage experimentation and learning, leaders can unlock the full potential of their workforce. This not only drives individual growth but also fuels organizational innovation and competitiveness.

The new leadership paradigms of post-postmodernism, metamodernism, and digimodernism offer a comprehensive framework for navigating the complexities of the contemporary business world. By embracing these approaches, leaders can develop the skills and mindset needed to drive sustainable success, foster innovation, and create ethical, inclusive, and resilient organizations. This book provides the insights and tools necessary for leaders to implement these strategies effectively, ensuring their businesses are well-equipped for the future.

The primary objective of this book is to provide both practical and theoretical insights into the emerging paradigm of post-postmodern leadership. By exploring the principles of post-postmodernism, metamodernism, and digimodernism, the book aims to equip business leaders with the tools and understanding necessary to navigate the complexities of the modern organizational landscape.

Readers will gain a comprehensive understanding of how these contemporary frameworks can be applied to enhance leadership effectiveness. The book delves into the intricacies of ethical leadership, adaptive strategies, and the integration of technology, offering actionable advice and real-world examples that illustrate how these concepts can be implemented in various business contexts.

The book aims to bridge the gap between traditional leadership models and the demands of today's rapidly evolving business environment. It emphasizes the importance of cultural sensitivity, employee empowerment, and collaborative networks, providing leaders with strategies to foster innovation, inclusivity, and resilience within their organizations.

Through a blend of theoretical exploration and practical application, the book seeks to inspire leaders to embrace a more nuanced, flexible, and ethically grounded approach. By adopting the insights and strategies presented, leaders will be better prepared to address the challenges of the 21st-century business world, driving their organizations toward sustainable success and growth.

This book introduces the principles of post-postmodernism, metamodernism, and digimodernism, offering fresh, practical strategies for modern leaders. Our goal is to equip you with the tools and insights necessary to navigate and thrive in this complex environment. We begin by examining why new leadership paradigms are essential and outline the key themes and chapters that will guide our exploration.

Chapter 1: Understanding Post-Postmodernism

Our journey starts with understanding the evolution of post-postmodernism. We explore its roots in response to the limitations of postmodernism, focusing on how it addresses the fragmented and fluid nature of contemporary organizations. By delving into the core concepts and significance of post-postmodernism, metamodernism, and digimodernism, we lay a foundation for why these frameworks are vital for today's business leaders.

Chapter 2: Emphasis on Networks and Relationships

The rigid hierarchies of the past are giving way to dynamic networks. We delve into how modern organizations function as interconnected webs of relationships and why this shift is crucial. You will learn about the role of individuals and teams within these networks and discover strategies for building and maintaining trust and collaboration in your organization.

Chapter 3: Ethical Considerations in Leadership

Ethics are at the forefront of contemporary leadership. Moving beyond traditional deontological approaches, we introduce principles of metamodern ethics that are flexible, context-sensitive, and responsive. Through real-world case studies, we demonstrate how to develop and implement ethical frameworks that resonate with today's stakeholders and foster a culture of integrity and accountability.

Chapter 4: New Forms of Power and Resistance

As organizations evolve, so do power dynamics. This chapter examines how traditional power structures are being challenged and redefined. We explore new modes of resistance and how to manage them constructively. You will learn methods to foster inclusive environments where diverse voices are heard and valued, leading to a more empowered and engaged workforce.

Chapter 5: The Integration of Play and Creativity

Incorporating elements of play and creativity into the workplace can drive innovation and employee engagement. We discuss the benefits of a playful work culture and offer techniques to foster creativity within your team. Practical strategies and activities are provided to help you create an environment where innovation thrives.

Chapter 6: Hybrid Approaches in Organizational Theory

Modern and postmodern elements can coexist in a hybrid organizational model. We explore the rationale behind integrating these approaches and provide steps for their implementation. By balancing innovation with tradition, you will learn how to create strategies that are adaptable and effective, ensuring your organization remains resilient in the face of change.

Chapter 7: Adapting to the Global Landscape

Globalization presents both challenges and opportunities. This chapter discusses how to navigate the global business environment with cultural sensitivity and adaptability. We provide tools for effective global collaboration and share examples of organizations that have successfully managed international teams and markets.

Conclusion: The Future of Post-Postmodern Leadership

We conclude by summarizing the key insights from the book and looking towards the future of post-postmodern leadership. Emerging trends and predictions are discussed, offering a forward-looking perspective. A practical call to action is provided, encouraging you to adopt and implement the metamodern strategies discussed, ensuring your organization is equipped for future success.

Appendices

To support your journey, we include detailed case studies of organizations that have successfully applied post-postmodern principles. Practical tools, including frameworks, exercises, and templates, are provided to help you implement these strategies in your organization. Additionally, an annotated bibliography of resources offers further reading for those interested in deepening their understanding of post-postmodernism in organizational theory.

Through this book, you will gain a comprehensive understanding of how to lead effectively in the modern business world, armed with the knowledge and tools to create ethical, innovative, and resilient organizations.

Chapter 1: Understanding Post-Postmodernism

To navigate the complexities of today's business environment, it is essential to understand the theoretical frameworks that underpin contemporary leadership paradigms. Post-postmodernism, metamodernism, and digimodernism represent a significant shift in how we view organizations and leadership. This chapter lays the groundwork by exploring the origins, core concepts, and significance of these frameworks.

The journey begins with a look at the historical context. The transition from modernism to postmodernism marked a profound shift in thought. Modernism, with its emphasis on progress, rationality, and universal truths, dominated the early 20th century. However, by the mid-20th century, cracks began to appear in this worldview. The rise of postmodernism challenged these notions, emphasizing skepticism, deconstruction, and the relativity of truth. Postmodernism critiqued the grand narratives and ideologies that had previously been taken for granted, highlighting the fragmented and subjective nature of reality.

As the limitations of postmodernism became evident, particularly its tendency toward cynicism and endless deconstruction, thinkers began to seek new ways to understand and engage with the world. This led to the development of post-postmodernism, or metamodernism, which aims to transcend the binaries of modernism and postmodernism by oscillating between them. It retains the critical insights of postmodernism but moves towards constructive and pragmatic solutions.

Key thinkers in this field include Timotheus Vermeulen and Robin van den Akker, who first articulated the concept of metamodernism in their seminal essay "Notes on Metamodernism." Their work builds on the ideas of earlier theorists like Jean-François Lyotard, who explored the limitations of modernist meta-narratives, and Fredric Jameson, who examined the cultural logic of late capitalism. These foundational texts provide a theoretical basis for understanding how post-postmodernism applies to organizational theory and leadership.

Post-postmodernism, metamodernism, and digimodernism each bring unique perspectives to the table. While they share common roots, it is important to distinguish between them:

- Post-postmodernism refers broadly to the philosophical and cultural developments that follow postmodernism, seeking to address its limitations and build on its insights.

- Metamodernism specifically describes the oscillation between modernist and postmodernist sensibilities, embracing both irony and sincerity, order and chaos, optimism and skepticism.

- Digimodernism focuses on the impact of digital technology on culture and society, highlighting how digital tools and platforms reshape our interactions and organizational structures.

Fundamental principles of these frameworks include a recognition of complexity and ambiguity, a rejection of absolute truths, and an emphasis on ethical and adaptive approaches to leadership. They advocate for a balance between pragmatism and idealism, encouraging leaders to be flexible, responsive, and culturally aware.

Post-postmodernism addresses several critical limitations of modernism and postmodernism in organizational theory. Modernist approaches often relied on rigid hierarchies and universal solutions, failing to account for the nuanced and dynamic nature of contemporary organizations. Postmodernism, while offering valuable critiques, frequently devolved into cynicism and fragmentation, providing little in the way of constructive frameworks for action.

By contrast, post-postmodernism offers a more balanced and practical approach. It acknowledges the complexity and fluidity of modern organizations while striving to create coherent and actionable strategies. This is particularly relevant in today's business environment, where leaders must navigate constant change, global interconnectedness, and diverse cultural contexts.

In contemporary organizational challenges, post-postmodernism provides tools for ethical decision-making, adaptive leadership, and the integration of technology. It encourages leaders to build networks and relationships rather than rely on top-down hierarchies. This framework supports the development of organizations that are resilient, innovative, and capable of thriving in an unpredictable world.

As we proceed through the book, the principles and strategies derived from post-postmodernism, metamodernism, and digimodernism will serve as a foundation for exploring new models of leadership. These models will be illustrated through real-world examples, case studies, and practical tools that you can apply to your organization. Understanding these theoretical underpinnings is the first step in becoming a more effective and forward-thinking leader.

The evolution of thought from modernism to postmodernism and beyond is a fascinating journey that reflects the changing complexities of society and, by extension, organizational theory and leadership. To grasp the significance of post-postmodernism, it's essential to understand this historical context.

Modernism, which emerged in the late 19th and early 20th centuries, was characterized by a belief in progress, rationality, and universal truths. It was an era marked by confidence in science, technology, and the power of human reason to solve problems and create a better future. Modernist thinkers and leaders favored grand narratives and overarching theories that provided clear, structured explanations of the world.

However, by the mid-20th century, disillusionment with these grand narratives began to grow. The horrors of two World Wars, economic depressions, and the complexities of an increasingly globalized world highlighted the limitations of modernist thinking. Enter postmodernism, which emerged as a reaction against the certainties of modernism.

Postmodernism took hold in the late 20th century, characterized by skepticism, relativism, and a focus on deconstruction. Postmodern thinkers like Jean-François Lyotard challenged the idea of universal truths, arguing that knowledge and reality are socially constructed and subject to change. Postmodernism emphasized the fragmented and subjective nature of human experience, celebrating diversity and plurality while questioning established power structures and ideologies.

In organizational theory, postmodernism led to a reevaluation of hierarchical structures and standardized practices. It encouraged leaders to embrace diversity, question authority, and recognize the multiplicity of perspectives within an organization. However, this critical stance often led to cynicism and paralysis, where the focus on deconstruction left little room for building constructive frameworks.

Recognizing these limitations, thinkers in the early 21st century began to seek a new approach. This led to the development of post-postmodernism or metamodernism. Pioneered by scholars like Timotheus Vermeulen and Robin van den Akker, metamodernism acknowledges the insights of postmodernism but moves beyond its skepticism. It oscillates between modernist optimism and postmodernist irony, aiming to create a balanced and dynamic perspective.

Post-postmodernism or metamodernism is characterized by a willingness to engage with grand narratives once more, but with a critical awareness of their limitations. It embraces complexity and contradiction, allowing for a synthesis of ideas that can lead to innovative and pragmatic solutions. In the realm of leadership, this translates to an approach that is flexible, responsive, and ethically grounded.

As we dive deeper into the book, we will explore how these historical shifts have shaped contemporary organizational theory and leadership practices. Understanding the transition from modernism to postmodernism and the emergence of post-postmodernism provides a crucial backdrop for appreciating the new paradigms of leadership that are emerging in response to today's challenges. This historical context sets the stage for a deeper exploration of how these ideas can be applied in practical, actionable ways to lead effectively in the modern business world.

The development of post-postmodernism, or metamodernism, has been shaped by the contributions of several key thinkers and foundational texts. These intellectual pioneers have provided the theoretical groundwork that informs contemporary understandings of organizational theory and leadership within this framework.

Timotheus Vermeulen and Robin van den Akker

Timotheus Vermeulen and Robin van den Akker are widely regarded as the primary architects of metamodernism. In their seminal essay, "Notes on Metamodernism," published in 2010, they articulate the core principles of this new cultural paradigm. They describe metamodernism as an oscillation between modernist enthusiasm and postmodernist irony, capturing the duality of our contemporary cultural sensibility. Their work emphasizes the need for a renewed sense of hope, sincerity, and engagement, even as we remain critically aware of the limitations and contradictions inherent in these pursuits.

Jean-François Lyotard

Though primarily associated with postmodernism, Jean-François Lyotard's work has also influenced the development of post-postmodern thought. His book, "The Postmodern Condition: A Report on Knowledge" (1979), critiqued the grand narratives of modernism and highlighted the fragmented nature of contemporary knowledge. This critique laid the groundwork for the metamodern emphasis on navigating between grand narratives and critical awareness, acknowledging the limitations of both without fully rejecting either.

Frederic Jameson

Frederic Jameson's exploration of the cultural logic of late capitalism in his book "Postmodernism, or, The Cultural Logic of Late Capitalism" (1991) provides another foundational text for post-postmodernism. Jameson's analysis of postmodern culture's pervasive influence on contemporary life offers insights into the conditions that necessitate a move beyond postmodernism. His work helps frame the context in which metamodernism seeks to operate, offering strategies to re-engage with the cultural and social complexities of the present.

Linda Hutcheon

Linda Hutcheon's contributions, particularly through her book "The Politics of Postmodernism" (1989), have also influenced metamodernism. Hutcheon explores the interplay between parody and politics in postmodern culture, highlighting the potential for new forms of engagement and meaning-making. This aligns with metamodernism's focus on sincerity and constructive approaches to culture and leadership.

Zygmunt Bauman

Zygmunt Bauman's concept of "liquid modernity," detailed in his book "Liquid Modernity" (2000), offers valuable insights into the fluid and transient nature of contemporary life. Bauman's work underscores the need for adaptive and flexible leadership strategies that can navigate the uncertainties of a constantly changing world, a central theme in metamodern organizational theory.

Alan Kirby

Alan Kirby's "Digimodernism: How New Technologies Dismantle the Postmodern and Reconfigure Our Culture" (2009) is a critical text for understanding the role of digital technology in post-postmodern thought. Kirby argues that digital media and technology have fundamentally altered cultural production and consumption, leading to new forms of engagement and interaction. His work highlights the importance of digital literacy and adaptability in contemporary leadership.

Robert Samuels

Robert Samuels' "New Media, Cultural Studies, and Critical Theory after Postmodernism: Automodernity from Zizek to Laclau" (2009) examines the intersection of new media and cultural theory, providing further context for understanding metamodernism. Samuels explores how digital technologies and cultural studies intersect with and move beyond postmodernism, offering insights into the new forms of social and organizational structures emerging in the digital age.

These key thinkers and foundational texts provide a rich intellectual backdrop for the development of post-postmodernism, metamodernism, and digimodernism. Their contributions offer valuable insights into the complexities of contemporary culture and organizational life, guiding the principles and practices that inform modern leadership strategies. As we proceed through this book, we will draw on these foundational ideas to explore practical applications and strategies for effective leadership in the 21st century.

Understanding the nuances and distinctions between post-postmodernism, metamodernism, and digimodernism is crucial for grasping their implications for contemporary leadership and organizational theory. Each of these frameworks offers unique insights while sharing common roots in their response to the limitations of modernism and postmodernism.

Post-Postmodernism

Post-postmodernism broadly refers to the cultural and intellectual movements that seek to move beyond the deconstructive tendencies of postmodernism. It is an umbrella term that encompasses various approaches aimed at reconstructing meaning, coherence, and purpose in a world perceived as fragmented and uncertain.

Definition: Post-postmodernism is a cultural and philosophical framework that arises as a response to the perceived shortcomings of postmodernism. It seeks to integrate the critical insights of postmodernism while striving for constructive and practical solutions.

Characteristics: It emphasizes pragmatism, ethical considerations, and a renewed sense of purpose. Post-postmodernism acknowledges complexity and ambiguity but aims to find coherence and actionable strategies amidst this uncertainty.

Metamodernism

Metamodernism is a specific manifestation of post-postmodernism. It is characterized by its oscillation between modernist and postmodernist sensibilities, capturing the duality of contemporary cultural experiences. Metamodernism seeks to harmonize the optimism and order of modernism with the skepticism and irony of postmodernism.

Definition: Metamodernism is a cultural and philosophical approach that oscillates between the ideals of modernism and the critiques of postmodernism, seeking a balanced and dynamic engagement with both.

Characteristics: It embraces irony and sincerity, hope and doubt, order and chaos. This oscillation allows for a flexible and adaptive mindset, capable of navigating the complexities of contemporary life. Metamodernism encourages leaders to be both pragmatic and visionary, blending practicality with creativity and ethical considerations.

Digimodernism

Digimodernism focuses on the transformative impact of digital technology on culture, society, and organizational structures. It highlights how digital tools and platforms are reshaping interactions, production, and consumption, leading to new forms of engagement and understanding.

Definition: Digimodernism is a cultural and philosophical framework that emphasizes the role of digital technology in transforming contemporary culture and society. It examines how digital advancements influence and reshape our ways of thinking and organizing.

Characteristics: Digimodernism underscores the importance of digital literacy and adaptability. It recognizes the pervasive influence of digital media and technology in everyday life and organizational contexts. This framework stresses the need for leaders to integrate digital tools into their strategies, fostering innovation and efficiency.

While post-postmodernism, metamodernism, and digimodernism share common themes, they each focus on different aspects of contemporary cultural and organizational dynamics:

- Scope and Focus: Post-postmodernism serves as a broad umbrella term encompassing various approaches that move beyond postmodernism. Metamodernism specifically describes the oscillation between modernist and postmodernist sensibilities, while digimodernism concentrates on the impact of digital technology.

- Cultural Engagement: Metamodernism emphasizes a balance between irony and sincerity, navigating the dualities of hope and skepticism. Digimodernism focuses on how digital technology reshapes cultural engagement and organizational structures.

- Application in Leadership: Post-postmodernism and metamodernism both encourage ethical, adaptive, and flexible leadership. Digimodernism adds a layer of technological integration, highlighting the importance of digital tools and strategies in modern leadership.

These frameworks collectively inform a more nuanced and comprehensive approach to leadership and organizational theory. By understanding their definitions and distinctions, leaders can develop strategies that are:

- Pragmatic and Constructive: Moving beyond mere critique to build actionable solutions.

- Ethically Grounded: Integrating ethical considerations into all aspects of leadership.

- Adaptable and Flexible: Embracing complexity and ambiguity with a dynamic and responsive mindset.

- Technologically Savvy: Leveraging digital tools and platforms to drive innovation and efficiency.

In the following chapters, we will explore how these principles can be applied in practical contexts, offering concrete examples and strategies for leading in a post-postmodern, metamodern, and digimodern world. By synthesizing these insights, leaders can navigate the complexities of the contemporary business environment with greater agility, creativity, and ethical integrity.

Leaders must embrace the complexity and ambiguity inherent in contemporary organizations. Flexible decision-making processes allow for adjustments as new information emerges, while adaptive strategies evolve in response to changing circumstances. Encouraging a culture of experimentation, where failure is seen as a learning opportunity, fosters innovation and continuous improvement.

Balancing pragmatism with visionary thinking is crucial. Leaders should articulate a compelling vision for the future while remaining grounded in practical realities. This involves setting ambitious goals but also being realistic about the steps needed to achieve them. Engaging sincerely with teams and stakeholders builds trust and inspires collective action.

Ethical considerations are central to effective leadership. Leaders must integrate ethics into their decision-making processes and organizational culture. Developing and implementing ethical frameworks guide decisions at all levels, considering the broader impact on society and the environment. Emphasizing corporate social responsibility (CSR) initiatives that align with company values enhances reputation and builds long-term stakeholder trust. A culture of transparency and accountability, where leaders are open about challenges and successes, builds credibility and trust.

Moving away from top-down hierarchical models, contemporary leadership emphasizes distributed and collaborative approaches. Leaders should empower teams to make decisions, creating an environment where employees feel valued and encouraged to take initiative. Developing collaborative networks within and outside the organization, fostering cross-functional teams and partnerships, leverages diverse perspectives and expertise. Inclusive leadership ensures that diverse voices are heard and respected, enhancing creativity and ensuring the organization benefits from a wide range of viewpoints.

Integrating technology and embracing digital transformation are essential. Leaders must be digitally literate, understanding the potential and limitations of various technologies. Leveraging data-driven insights informs decision-making, necessitating investment in data analytics and ensuring data is accessible and actionable. Embracing digital tools and platforms enhances productivity and innovation, streamlining operations, improving customer experiences, and creating new business opportunities.

Cultural sensitivity and a global mindset are crucial in an interconnected world. Leaders should develop an understanding of different cultural contexts and practices, enhancing the ability to manage diverse teams and engage with international markets effectively. Strategies should be adaptable to different cultural and economic contexts, being responsive to local needs while maintaining a cohesive global vision. Encouraging cross-cultural competence within the organization through training and development programs fosters a more inclusive and effective workplace.

Fostering creativity and innovation is essential for staying competitive. Designing workspaces that inspire creativity and collaboration, and implementing programs that encourage innovation, such as hackathons and innovation labs, generate new ideas and bring them to market quickly. Recognizing and rewarding creative contributions and innovative thinking reinforces a culture of innovation and motivates employees to continue pushing boundaries.

By integrating these principles, business leaders can create organizations that are resilient, adaptable, ethical, innovative, and globally competitive, ensuring their businesses thrive in the complex and rapidly evolving landscape of the 21st century.

Post-postmodernism emerges as a response to the limitations of both modernism and postmodernism, providing a more balanced and dynamic framework for understanding and leading contemporary organizations. By addressing the shortcomings of these earlier paradigms, post-postmodernism offers practical solutions that are better suited to the complexities of the modern business environment.

Modernism, with its emphasis on progress, rationality, and universal truths, often failed to account for the nuanced and diverse realities of human experience. Its focus on grand narratives and rigid structures left little room for flexibility and adaptation, making it difficult to respond effectively to rapid changes and complex problems. In contrast, post-postmodernism acknowledges the importance of structure and progress but does so with a critical awareness of their limitations. It embraces complexity and ambiguity, allowing for more flexible and adaptive approaches to problem-solving and decision-making.

Postmodernism, which emerged as a critique of modernism, brought valuable insights into the fragmented and subjective nature of reality. It challenged the idea of universal truths and highlighted the importance of diverse perspectives. However, its focus on deconstruction and skepticism often led to cynicism and paralysis, with little room for constructive action. Post-postmodernism retains the critical awareness of postmodernism but moves beyond its skepticism. It seeks to balance critique with constructive engagement, allowing for the development of practical and actionable strategies that can address real-world challenges.

One of the key ways post-postmodernism addresses the limitations of both modernism and postmodernism is through its emphasis on ethical considerations. Modernism's focus on efficiency and progress sometimes overlooked the ethical implications of actions, while postmodernism's relativism often made it difficult to establish clear ethical guidelines. Post-postmodernism integrates ethics into its core principles, promoting ethical decision-making and corporate social responsibility. This ensures that leaders not only strive for efficiency and innovation but also consider the broader impact of their actions on society and the environment.

Post-postmodernism also emphasizes the importance of distributed and collaborative leadership. Modernist hierarchies often stifled creativity and innovation, while postmodernism's critique of authority sometimes led to a lack of coherent leadership. By promoting collaborative and networked approaches, post-postmodernism allows for more inclusive and participatory leadership models. This encourages diverse voices and perspectives, fostering a culture of innovation and collective problem-solving.

With this framework we recognize the transformative impact of digital technology, something that both modernism and postmodernism struggled to fully integrate. Modernist approaches often failed to anticipate the rapid advancements in technology, while postmodernism critiqued but did not fully engage with the digital revolution. Post-postmodernism, particularly through the lens of digimodernism, embraces digital transformation, highlighting the need for digital literacy and the integration of technology into all aspects of business operations. This ensures that organizations remain competitive and innovative in a technologically advanced landscape.

Cultural sensitivity is another area where post-postmodernism addresses the limitations of its predecessors. Modernist universalism often ignored cultural differences, while postmodernism's focus on fragmentation sometimes led to an inability to navigate cultural complexities effectively. Post-postmodernism promotes cultural sensitivity and a global mindset, encouraging leaders to understand and navigate diverse cultural contexts. This enhances the ability to manage international teams and engage with global markets, making organizations more effective in a globalized world.

Post-postmodernism addresses the limitations of modernism and postmodernism by embracing complexity and ambiguity, integrating ethical considerations, promoting collaborative leadership, leveraging digital technology, and fostering cultural sensitivity. These principles provide a more balanced and dynamic framework for contemporary leadership, enabling organizations to navigate the complexities of the modern business environment with greater agility, creativity, and ethical integrity. It provides a vital framework for addressing the multifaceted challenges contemporary organizations face. Its principles offer practical solutions that align with the complexities of today's business environment. Here are some key areas where post-postmodernism is particularly relevant, along with examples of how organizations can apply its insights:

Navigating Complexity and Ambiguity

Contemporary organizations operate in an environment characterized by rapid change and uncertainty. Post-postmodernism's emphasis on embracing complexity and ambiguity helps leaders navigate these conditions effectively. For example, in the technology sector, companies like Google and Amazon thrive by adopting flexible and adaptive strategies. These organizations foster a culture of continuous learning and experimentation, allowing them to pivot quickly in response to market changes and technological advancements.

Ethical Leadership and Corporate Social Responsibility

As stakeholders increasingly demand ethical behavior and social responsibility, post-postmodernism's focus on integrating ethics into leadership is crucial. Patagonia, an outdoor apparel company, exemplifies this approach. The company is known for its commitment to environmental sustainability and ethical practices. By integrating these values into their business model, Patagonia not only enhances its brand reputation but also attracts a loyal customer base that shares its values.

Distributed and Collaborative Leadership

The shift away from hierarchical structures toward more collaborative and networked approaches is another area where post-postmodernism is relevant. For instance, Valve Corporation, a video game developer, operates with a flat organizational structure where employees are encouraged to take ownership of projects and collaborate across teams. This distributed leadership model fosters innovation and empowers employees to contribute their best ideas, leading to highly creative and successful products.

Leveraging Digital Technology

In today's digital age, the ability to effectively integrate technology into business operations is essential. Post-postmodernism, through the lens of digimodernism, highlights the transformative impact of digital tools. Companies like Netflix have revolutionized their industries by leveraging data analytics and digital platforms. Netflix uses sophisticated algorithms to personalize content recommendations for its users, enhancing customer satisfaction and engagement.

Cultural Sensitivity and Globalization

As businesses expand globally, cultural sensitivity becomes increasingly important. Post-postmodernism's emphasis on understanding and navigating diverse cultural contexts is crucial for global success. For example, Starbucks has successfully adapted its business model to various cultural contexts around the world. By understanding local preferences and cultural nuances, Starbucks tailors its offerings and store experiences to meet the unique needs of each market, enhancing its global appeal.

Innovation and Creativity

Encouraging creativity and innovation is essential for staying competitive. Post-postmodernism's integration of play and creativity into the workplace can drive significant business success. Google's "20% time" policy, which allows employees to spend 20% of their work time on projects they are passionate about, has led to the development of highly successful products like Gmail and Google Maps. This policy exemplifies how fostering a creative work environment can lead to groundbreaking innovations.

Many organizations adopt agile methodologies to manage projects and workflows. Agile practices, which emphasize iterative development and flexibility, align well with post-postmodern principles. For example, software development companies use agile frameworks like Scrum to manage complex projects, allowing them to respond quickly to changes and deliver high-quality products.

Organizations are increasingly implementing ethical decision-making frameworks to guide their operations. For instance, Unilever's Sustainable Living Plan integrates sustainability into its business strategy, aiming to double the size of the business while reducing its environmental footprint and increasing its positive social impact. The use of collaborative platforms like Slack and Microsoft Teams facilitates distributed leadership and enhances communication across teams. These tools enable real-time collaboration, breaking down silos and fostering a more inclusive and connected organizational culture.

Companies are leveraging big data and analytics to inform their strategies and operations. For example, retail giant Walmart uses data analytics to optimize its supply chain, manage inventory, and enhance customer experiences. This data-driven approach helps Walmart stay competitive in a rapidly changing market. Organizations are developing global talent management strategies to attract and retain diverse talent. For instance, IBM's global workforce programs focus on cultural sensitivity and inclusivity, ensuring that employees from diverse backgrounds feel valued and empowered.

By applying the principles of post-postmodernism, organizations can effectively address contemporary challenges, fostering environments that are adaptable, innovative, and ethically grounded. These examples illustrate how post-postmodern frameworks can lead to more resilient and successful businesses in the modern landscape.

Chapter 2: Emphasis on Networks and Relationships

Traditional rigid hierarchies that once defined organizations are being replaced by more dynamic and flexible networks. This shift is reshaping how companies operate, encouraging a more interconnected and collaborative approach to management. In this chapter, we explore the significance of networks and relationships in modern organizational structures and examine how businesses can leverage these networks for greater success.

The move from rigid hierarchies to flexible networks reflects the need for organizations to be more adaptive and responsive to change. Companies like Google and Valve Corporation serve as prime examples of networked organizations that thrive on flexibility and innovation. These organizations demonstrate how dynamic networks can enhance creativity, speed up decision-making processes, and improve overall efficiency.

At the heart of these networks are individuals and teams whose roles and interactions are crucial to the organization's success. Understanding the dynamics of these interconnected actors is essential for fostering a collaborative and productive work environment. Strategies for promoting effective collaboration and communication within these networks will be explored, highlighting the importance of creating spaces where ideas can flow freely and teamwork is encouraged.

Building and maintaining strong relationships within and outside the organization is fundamental to sustaining these networks. Trust and reciprocity form the foundation of successful professional relationships. In this chapter, we will delve into the importance of these elements and provide tools and practices for nurturing them. By emphasizing trust and fostering a culture of reciprocity, organizations can create more cohesive and resilient networks.

Through case studies and practical examples, this chapter will illustrate how businesses can effectively transition to and manage networked structures. The insights gained will help leaders understand the benefits of dynamic networks and equip them with the knowledge to cultivate and maintain these relationships, ultimately driving their organizations toward greater innovation and success.

The contemporary business landscape is marked by rapid change, technological advancements, and increasing complexity. In response to these challenges, many organizations are moving away from traditional rigid hierarchies and embracing more flexible networked structures. This shift is not merely a change in organizational charts but represents a fundamental transformation in how businesses operate and succeed.

Rigid hierarchies, characterized by top-down decision-making and clearly defined roles, have long been the standard model for organizing work. While this structure can provide clarity and control, it often stifles innovation, slows down decision-making, and fails to adapt quickly to new market demands. The hierarchical approach tends to create silos, where information and resources are not easily shared across departments, leading to inefficiencies and missed opportunities.

In contrast, dynamic networks prioritize flexibility, adaptability, and interconnectivity. These networks are composed of interconnected actors—individuals, teams, and even external partners—who collaborate and share information freely. This approach fosters a more agile and responsive organization, capable of quickly adapting to changes and seizing new opportunities.

A prime example of this shift can be seen in the technology sector, where companies like Google have adopted networked structures to great effect. Google's organizational model encourages cross-functional collaboration and empowers employees to take initiative. This networked approach has been instrumental in driving innovation and maintaining the company's competitive edge.

Another example is Valve Corporation, a video game developer known for its flat organizational structure. Valve operates without formal job titles or rigid hierarchies, allowing employees to work on projects that align with their interests and expertise. This flexibility has led to a highly creative and motivated workforce, capable of producing groundbreaking products in a highly competitive industry.

The success of these companies highlights the advantages of dynamic networks. By breaking down traditional silos, networked organizations facilitate faster decision-making and more effective problem-solving. The open flow of information and resources enables teams to collaborate more efficiently, leading to higher levels of innovation and productivity.

Transitioning to a networked structure is not without its challenges. It requires a cultural shift that embraces collaboration, trust, and shared responsibility. Leaders must be willing to relinquish some control and empower employees to take ownership of their work. This shift also necessitates new management practices and tools to support effective communication and collaboration across the network.

The move from rigid hierarchies to flexible networks represents a significant evolution in organizational design. By embracing dynamic networks, businesses can become more agile, innovative, and resilient in the face of change. As we delve deeper into this chapter, we will explore the specific strategies and practices that can help organizations successfully navigate this transition, fostering a more interconnected and collaborative environment.

Case Studies of Networked Organizations

Spotify

Spotify, the music streaming giant, has also adopted a networked approach known as the "Spotify Model." This model is characterized by the use of "squads," small, cross-functional teams that operate autonomously. Each squad is akin to a mini-startup, empowered to make decisions and innovate rapidly. These squads are part of larger "tribes" that work on related areas, ensuring alignment and coordination without sacrificing flexibility. This structure allows Spotify to continuously improve its platform and respond quickly to user feedback and technological changes.

Zappos

Zappos, the online shoe and clothing retailer, implemented a networked structure through a management approach called Holacracy. This system replaces traditional hierarchies with a series of self-organizing teams called circles. Each circle operates with a high degree of autonomy, making decisions and managing their workflows independently. This approach has allowed Zappos to maintain its customer-centric focus and agility, even as it has grown significantly. The flexibility and empowerment provided by Holacracy have been key to Zappos' ability to innovate and maintain a strong company culture.

Buurtzorg

Buurtzorg, a Dutch home-care organization, provides an exemplary case of networked structures in a non-tech environment. The organization operates with small, self-managing teams of nurses who have the autonomy to make decisions about patient care. This networked approach has led to high levels of patient satisfaction and efficiency. By empowering nurses to manage their workloads and collaborate directly with patients and each other, Buurtzorg has reduced administrative overhead and improved the quality of care.

Haier

Haier, a leading global appliance manufacturer based in China, has revolutionized its organizational structure by adopting a model known as the Rendanheyi Model. This approach transforms the company into a network of micro-enterprises, each with its own profit and loss statement, operating almost like independent startups. These micro-enterprises are highly autonomous, with the freedom to innovate and respond quickly to market changes. This networked structure has allowed Haier to stay competitive and agile in the fast-paced consumer electronics industry.

W.L. Gore & Associates

W.L. Gore & Associates, the company behind GORE-TEX products, is renowned for its unique lattice organizational structure. Instead of traditional hierarchies, Gore operates with a network of interconnected teams, where leadership emerges based on knowledge, skills, and the ability to influence rather than formal titles. This egalitarian approach fosters a strong culture of innovation and collaboration. Teams at Gore are empowered to make decisions, which has been key to the company's sustained innovation and market leadership in advanced materials.

Morning Star

Morning Star, a leading tomato processing company, operates with a self-management model. Every employee, referred to as a "colleague," has the freedom to take on any role and is responsible for creating their own mission statements that align with the company's goals. This approach removes traditional managerial roles and fosters a culture of accountability and empowerment. By eliminating rigid hierarchies, Morning Star has created a highly efficient and motivated workforce, leading to continuous improvements in productivity and innovation.

GitHub

GitHub, a platform for software development and version control, utilizes a flat organizational structure that emphasizes collaboration and transparency. Employees at GitHub work in small, self-organizing teams that are free to choose the projects they want to work on. This autonomy promotes creativity and innovation, allowing GitHub to rapidly develop new features and respond to the needs of its user community. The company's open communication culture, where information is shared freely across all levels, enhances coordination and collective problem-solving.

Whole Foods Market

Whole Foods Market employs a decentralized team-based structure, where each store operates as a semi-autonomous unit. Within each store, employees are organized into teams that manage different departments, such as produce or bakery. These teams have significant decision-making authority, including the ability to influence hiring and inventory decisions. This networked approach empowers employees to take ownership of their work and respond more effectively to customer needs, contributing to Whole Foods' reputation for high-quality products and customer service.

In networked organizations, the roles of individuals and teams are fundamentally different from those in traditional hierarchical structures. The shift to a more interconnected model emphasizes collaboration, flexibility, and shared responsibility, transforming how work is done and how success is achieved.

Individuals in networked organizations are empowered to take on multiple roles and responsibilities, often crossing traditional departmental boundaries. This flexibility allows employees to contribute in various capacities, fostering a more dynamic and engaging work environment. For example, at companies like Haier and Morning Star, employees are encouraged to take ownership of their projects and pursue initiatives that align with their strengths and interests. This empowerment not only boosts morale but also drives innovation, as individuals feel more invested in the outcomes of their work.

Teams in networked organizations operate with a high degree of autonomy. They are often self-organizing, meaning they have the authority to make decisions and manage their workflows independently. This autonomy is crucial for fostering creativity and rapid problem-solving. At Spotify, for instance, the concept of "squads" allows small, cross-functional teams to function as independent units with their own goals and responsibilities. These squads can quickly adapt to changes and experiment with new ideas without needing approval from higher levels of management.

Collaboration is a cornerstone of networked organizations. Effective collaboration requires open communication, trust, and mutual respect among team members. Tools like Slack, Microsoft Teams, and Trello facilitate real-time communication and project management, making it easier for teams to stay connected and coordinated. At W.L. Gore & Associates, the lattice structure supports fluid communication channels, enabling employees to collaborate across teams and departments seamlessly.

The interconnected nature of these organizations also means that individuals and teams are often part of broader networks that extend beyond the company. Partnerships with external stakeholders, such as customers, suppliers, and other businesses, are integral to the organization's success. For example, GitHub's platform thrives on its extensive community of developers who contribute to open-source projects and collaborate on software development. This external network enhances GitHub's capabilities and drives continuous innovation.

Building and maintaining trust is essential in networked organizations. Trust enables individuals and teams to take risks, share ideas freely, and support one another in achieving common goals. Organizations like Valve Corporation emphasize trust in their culture, allowing employees to choose the projects they want to work on and collaborate with others based on mutual respect and shared interests. This trust-based approach leads to higher job satisfaction and more effective teamwork.

The role of leadership in networked organizations shifts from command-and-control to facilitation and support. Leaders are tasked with creating an environment that encourages collaboration, innovation, and personal growth. They act as mentors and coaches, providing guidance and resources while allowing teams the freedom to navigate their paths. At Whole Foods Market, team leaders focus on empowering their teams to make decisions and take initiative, fostering a sense of ownership and accountability among employees.

Professional development and continuous learning are also vital in networked organizations. Individuals are encouraged to expand their skill sets and pursue new knowledge, often supported by the organization through training programs and learning opportunities. This focus on development ensures that employees remain adaptable and capable of contributing to the organization in diverse ways. For example, Google offers various programs and resources for employee development, encouraging continuous growth and innovation.

The role of individuals and teams within networked organizations is characterized by empowerment, autonomy, collaboration, and continuous learning. These elements are essential for fostering a dynamic and innovative work environment that can adapt to the complexities of the modern business landscape. By embracing these principles, organizations can harness the collective strengths of their employees, drive innovation, and achieve sustained success.

Fostering effective collaboration and communication is crucial for the success of networked organizations. The interconnected nature of these organizations relies on seamless interaction and shared understanding among team members. Here are some key strategies to enhance collaboration and communication within such environments:

Establish Clear Goals and Expectations

Setting clear goals and expectations is fundamental to effective collaboration. Teams need a shared understanding of what they are working towards and the standards by which success will be measured. Clear goals provide direction and help align individual efforts with organizational objectives. For example, Spotify's "squads" set their goals aligned with the company's broader mission, ensuring coherence and focus across the organization.

Utilize Collaborative Tools

Leveraging digital tools can significantly enhance communication and collaboration. Platforms like Slack, Microsoft Teams, and Trello facilitate real-time communication, project management, and document sharing. These tools help keep team members connected, organized, and informed. At GitHub, the use of collaborative platforms allows developers to work together on projects seamlessly, regardless of their physical location.

Foster a Culture of Openness and Trust

Creating a culture where team members feel safe to share ideas, ask questions, and provide feedback is essential for effective collaboration. This involves promoting transparency and open communication at all levels of the organization. Companies like Valve Corporation prioritize trust and openness, encouraging employees to communicate freely and collaborate based on mutual respect and shared goals.

Encourage Cross-Functional Teams

Forming cross-functional teams that bring together diverse skills and perspectives can drive innovation and problem-solving. These teams can approach challenges from various angles, leading to more comprehensive and creative solutions. For instance, at Google, cross-functional teams are common, allowing for diverse input and collaboration across different areas of expertise.

Implement Regular Check-Ins and Meetings

Regular check-ins and meetings help maintain alignment and ensure that team members are on the same page. These meetings provide opportunities to discuss progress, address challenges, and adjust plans as needed. Agile practices, such as daily stand-up meetings used by many tech companies, ensure continuous communication and quick resolution of issues.

Provide Training and Development

Investing in training and development programs enhances team members' collaboration and communication skills. Workshops on effective communication, conflict resolution, and teamwork can equip employees with the tools they need to collaborate more effectively. At Whole Foods Market, continuous training ensures that team members are equipped with the skills necessary for effective collaboration.

Promote Inclusivity and Diversity

Creating an inclusive environment where diverse voices are heard and valued is crucial for effective collaboration. Encouraging diversity of thought and experience leads to richer discussions and better decision-making. Organizations like W.L. Gore & Associates embrace inclusivity, ensuring that all employees feel empowered to contribute their unique perspectives.

Encourage Feedback and Continuous Improvement

Establishing a feedback-rich environment helps teams continuously improve their collaboration processes. Regularly soliciting and acting on feedback ensures that communication channels remain effective and that any issues are promptly addressed. Companies like Haier emphasize continuous improvement and feedback, allowing their micro-enterprises to adapt and enhance their collaboration practices.

Design Collaborative Workspaces

Physical and virtual workspaces designed to facilitate collaboration can enhance team interactions. Open office layouts, collaborative tools, and virtual meeting spaces all contribute to a more interactive and communicative work environment. For example, many innovative companies design their office spaces to include communal areas where spontaneous collaboration can occur.

Leadership Support and Facilitation

Leaders play a crucial role in fostering a collaborative environment. By modeling effective communication, encouraging teamwork, and providing the necessary resources, leaders can create a culture that values and supports collaboration. At Morning Star, leaders act as facilitators, guiding their teams and supporting their collaborative efforts without micromanaging.

Fostering effective collaboration and communication in networked organizations involves a multifaceted approach that includes clear goal-setting, leveraging collaborative tools, promoting a culture of openness and trust, and encouraging cross-functional teamwork. By implementing these strategies, organizations can enhance their collaborative capabilities, driving innovation and achieving greater success in today's complex business landscape.

Building and maintaining relationships in networked organizations hinges on the importance of trust and reciprocity. Trust is the foundation of any effective relationship, fostering an environment where individuals feel confident in relying on one another. In a business context, trust allows team members to communicate openly, share ideas, and collaborate without fear of undue criticism or hidden agendas. This openness is crucial for innovation, as it encourages the free exchange of thoughts and the willingness to take risks.

Reciprocity, the mutual exchange of favors and support, complements trust by reinforcing the interdependence among team members. When individuals know that their contributions will be recognized and reciprocated, they are more likely to invest in the success of their colleagues and the organization as a whole. This mutual support creates a positive feedback loop, where acts of cooperation and assistance build stronger, more cohesive teams.

For instance, in companies like Google and Valve Corporation, trust and reciprocity are integral to their operational models. Google's encouragement of "20% time" not only demonstrates trust in its employees' ability to manage their time and innovate but also fosters a culture where employees feel valued and supported. Similarly, Valve's flat organizational structure relies heavily on mutual trust among employees to choose and commit to projects, ensuring that everyone's efforts are directed towards common goals.

To build and sustain these relationships, organizations must prioritize transparency and consistent communication. Regular check-ins, open forums, and transparent decision-making processes help reinforce trust by keeping everyone informed and involved. Leaders play a pivotal role in modeling these behaviors, demonstrating transparency in their actions and decisions, and fostering an environment where trust can flourish.

Cultivating a culture of appreciation and recognition strengthens reciprocity. Acknowledging individual and team contributions reinforces the value of mutual support and encourages continued cooperation. At Zappos, for example, the company's focus on a positive workplace culture includes regular recognition of employee efforts, fostering a strong sense of community and shared purpose.

Providing opportunities for social interaction and team-building activities also enhances trust and reciprocity. Informal gatherings, team outings, and collaborative projects allow team members to build personal connections, which translate into stronger professional relationships. These interactions help individuals understand each other's strengths and challenges, promoting empathy and cooperation.

In virtual or remote work environments, maintaining trust and reciprocity can be more challenging but equally important. Organizations must leverage digital tools to facilitate continuous and meaningful communication. Video conferences, virtual team-building exercises, and collaborative online platforms can help bridge the gap, ensuring that team members remain connected and engaged.

Professional development opportunities further reinforce trust and reciprocity. When organizations invest in their employees' growth, it signals trust in their potential and a commitment to their success. This investment encourages employees to reciprocate with loyalty and dedication to the organization. Companies like Whole Foods Market, which emphasize continuous learning and development, benefit from highly engaged and committed teams.

Tools and practices for nurturing professional relationships in networked organizations are crucial for maintaining the fabric of trust and reciprocity that drives collaborative success. Digital communication platforms like Slack and Microsoft Teams facilitate real-time interaction and keep team members connected, regardless of their physical location. These tools enable seamless collaboration, allowing for instant messaging, video calls, and document sharing, which help maintain transparency and foster a sense of togetherness.

Another essential practice is the use of regular feedback mechanisms. Performance reviews, one-on-one meetings, and peer evaluations provide opportunities for constructive feedback and recognition. This continuous dialogue helps employees feel valued and heard, reinforcing their connection to the team and the organization. Additionally, anonymous surveys can be employed to gather honest feedback on organizational practices and team dynamics, helping leaders identify areas for improvement and demonstrating a commitment to continuous development.

Mentorship programs are also effective in nurturing professional relationships. Pairing less experienced employees with seasoned mentors creates a structured environment for knowledge sharing and personal growth. These relationships build trust and provide mentees with guidance and support, while mentors gain satisfaction from contributing to their colleagues' development.

Team-building activities, both virtual and in-person, play a significant role in fostering strong relationships. Activities that encourage teamwork, problem-solving, and communication help break down barriers and build rapport among team members. For instance, virtual escape rooms, hackathons, and collaborative workshops can create a sense of camaraderie and shared purpose.

Another practice is the establishment of communities of practice or interest groups within the organization. These groups bring together individuals with shared interests or professional goals, providing a platform for networking, learning, and support. Regular meetings and discussions within these groups foster deeper connections and encourage the exchange of ideas and best practices.

Celebrating milestones and achievements is also vital. Recognizing and celebrating individual and team successes, whether through formal awards, shout-outs during meetings, or social media highlights, reinforces a culture of appreciation. These celebrations not only boost morale but also strengthen the bonds among team members by acknowledging their contributions and shared victories.

Clear and open communication from leadership is essential. Leaders should regularly share updates on organizational goals, challenges, and successes. This transparency helps build trust and ensures that everyone is aligned with the organization's direction. Open-door policies, where employees feel comfortable approaching leaders with ideas or concerns, further enhance this trust.

Chapter 3: Ethical Considerations in Leadership

As the complexities of the modern business landscape continue to evolve, the role of ethics in leadership has never been more critical. Traditional ethical frameworks, often rooted in deontological principles, have guided business practices for decades. These frameworks, which emphasize rules, duties, and obligations, have provided a foundation for decision-making and corporate behavior. However, in the face of rapid technological advancements, global interconnectedness, and shifting societal expectations, these traditional approaches sometimes fall short.

In this chapter, we will explore the limitations of deontological ethics in addressing contemporary business challenges. We will introduce non-deontological approaches that offer more flexibility, context-sensitivity, and responsiveness—key characteristics of what we term metamodern ethics. By examining these principles, we aim to provide a nuanced understanding of how ethical considerations can be integrated into leadership practices in a way that is both practical and dynamic.

Developing ethical frameworks that align with metamodern principles involves creating guidelines that are adaptable to various contexts and capable of responding to the unique challenges that arise in today's business environment. We will delve into the processes and models that facilitate ethical decision-making, highlighting how leaders can navigate complex ethical dilemmas with a balanced and informed approach.

Practical applications are essential for understanding how these ethical principles can be effectively implemented. Through case studies, we will examine real-world scenarios where businesses have faced ethical dilemmas, exploring the decisions made and their outcomes. These examples will provide valuable insights into the application of metamodern ethics in resolving conflicts and guiding corporate behavior.

Embedding ethics into organizational culture is a crucial step in ensuring that ethical considerations are not merely theoretical but are lived and practiced daily. We will discuss best practices for fostering an ethical culture within organizations, emphasizing the importance of leadership, communication, and continuous reinforcement of ethical standards.

As we navigate through this chapter, our goal is to equip leaders with the tools and understanding necessary to develop and maintain ethical frameworks that are robust yet adaptable. By embracing metamodern ethics, leaders can make informed decisions that not only comply with traditional standards but also reflect the evolving values and expectations of a global society. In doing so, they can build organizations that are not only successful but also responsible and respected in the eyes of their stakeholders.

Traditional ethical frameworks in business have predominantly been shaped by deontological principles, which emphasize adherence to rules, duties, and obligations. Deontological ethics, rooted in the works of philosophers like Immanuel Kant, focuses on the inherent rightness or wrongness of actions themselves, rather than their consequences. This approach has provided a clear and structured way to guide ethical behavior in organizations. However, as businesses operate in increasingly complex and dynamic environments, the limitations of deontological ethics become apparent.

One significant critique of deontological ethics in business is its rigidity. The emphasis on strict adherence to predefined rules can be inflexible and may not account for the nuanced realities of contemporary business operations. For instance, a deontological approach might dictate that lying is always wrong. While this provides a clear ethical stance, it doesn't consider scenarios where lying might prevent harm or lead to a greater good. This black-and-white perspective can hinder leaders from making pragmatic decisions in complex situations where ethical dilemmas are not clear-cut.

Deontological ethics often fails to address the broader context in which business decisions are made. Businesses today operate in a globalized world with diverse cultural, social, and economic landscapes. A rigid set of rules may not be applicable or relevant across different contexts. For example, ethical norms and expectations can vary significantly between cultures. A deontological framework that works well in one cultural setting might be inappropriate or even harmful in another. This lack of context-sensitivity limits the applicability of deontological ethics in a global business environment.

Another limitation is the focus on individual actions without considering systemic and structural issues. Deontological ethics tends to evaluate the morality of individual decisions rather than the broader organizational practices and policies that shape those decisions. In a business context, many ethical issues arise not from individual actions but from systemic practices, such as corporate governance, labor policies, and supply chain management. A purely deontological approach may overlook these systemic factors, leading to ethical blind spots within the organization.

The deontological focus on duty and obligation can sometimes lead to ethical minimalism, where businesses do just enough to comply with rules and regulations without striving for higher ethical standards. This compliance-based mindset can prevent organizations from proactively addressing ethical challenges and fostering a culture of integrity and responsibility. In contrast, a more flexible and dynamic approach to ethics encourages continuous improvement and innovation in ethical practices.

The rapidly changing technological landscape poses challenges that traditional deontological ethics may struggle to address. Emerging technologies such as artificial intelligence, big data, and biotechnology introduce new ethical dilemmas that existing rules may not cover. For instance, issues related to data privacy, algorithmic bias, and genetic modification require ethical considerations that go beyond traditional frameworks. Leaders need an ethical approach that can adapt to new and unforeseen challenges, guiding decision-making in areas where established rules are lacking.

While deontological ethics has provided a foundational framework for business ethics, its limitations in flexibility, context-sensitivity, systemic consideration, and adaptability highlight the need for alternative approaches. As we move forward in this chapter, we will explore non-deontological approaches to ethics that offer greater flexibility and responsiveness, equipping leaders with the tools to navigate the complex ethical landscape of contemporary business. These approaches will provide a more nuanced and practical framework for ethical decision-making, better suited to the dynamic and interconnected world in which modern organizations operate.

In response to the limitations of deontological ethics, non-deontological approaches offer alternative frameworks that are more adaptable, context-sensitive, and responsive to the complexities of contemporary business environments. These approaches move beyond the rigid rule-based structure of deontology, providing a more flexible and pragmatic foundation for ethical decision-making in organizations.

One prominent non-deontological approach is consequentialism, which evaluates the morality of actions based on their outcomes rather than their adherence to predefined rules. Utilitarianism, a well-known form of consequentialism, posits that the rightness or wrongness of an action depends on its ability to produce the greatest good for the greatest number of people. This approach allows leaders to consider the broader impact of their decisions, weighing the potential benefits and harms to various stakeholders. For example, a company deciding to implement a new technology might use a utilitarian framework to assess how the change will affect employees, customers, shareholders, and the community, aiming to maximize overall well-being.

Virtue ethics, another non-deontological approach, emphasizes the importance of character and moral virtues over specific actions. Originating from the philosophy of Aristotle, virtue ethics focuses on the development of good character traits, such as honesty, courage, and empathy, which guide individuals in making ethical decisions. In a business context, virtue ethics encourages leaders to cultivate personal integrity and moral excellence, creating an organizational culture that prioritizes ethical behavior. For instance, a leader guided by virtue ethics might emphasize transparency and fairness in decision-making processes, fostering trust and respect within the organization.

Care ethics, which emerged from feminist philosophy, underscores the significance of relationships, empathy, and care in ethical decision-making. This approach highlights the interconnectedness of individuals and the moral importance of caring for others, especially those who are vulnerable. In business, care ethics can be applied to enhance employee well-being, customer relations, and community engagement. A company might implement policies that support work-life balance, provide comprehensive employee benefits, and engage in corporate social responsibility initiatives that address community needs.

Pragmatism offers another non-deontological perspective, focusing on practical outcomes and the continuous adaptation of ethical principles to changing circumstances. Pragmatic ethics rejects absolute rules and instead advocates for an iterative process of ethical inquiry and experimentation. This approach aligns well with the dynamic nature of modern business, where leaders must constantly adapt to new challenges and opportunities. For example, a pragmatic leader might pilot a new sustainability initiative, gather feedback, and make adjustments based on the results, continuously refining their approach to achieve the best possible ethical outcomes.

Postmodern ethics, influenced by postmodern philosophy, challenges the notion of universal moral truths and emphasizes the diversity of moral perspectives. This approach encourages leaders to be aware of and respect different cultural, social, and individual viewpoints, fostering a more inclusive and equitable organizational environment. In practice, postmodern ethics might lead a global corporation to tailor its business practices to align with the ethical norms and values of the diverse regions in which it operates, ensuring sensitivity and respect for local cultures.

Integrative social contracts theory combines elements of deontological and non-deontological approaches by emphasizing the role of implicit social agreements in ethical decision-making. This theory posits that ethical norms arise from the agreements and expectations within specific communities or societies. Leaders guided by this approach consider the implicit social contracts with their stakeholders, striving to honor these agreements and uphold the trust placed in them. For instance, a company might develop ethical guidelines based on the expectations of its employees, customers, and local communities, ensuring that its actions align with these collective values.

Non-deontological approaches offer valuable alternatives to traditional rule-based ethics, providing frameworks that are more adaptable, context-sensitive, and responsive to the complexities of contemporary business. By incorporating consequentialist, virtue ethics, care ethics, pragmatism, postmodern ethics, and integrative social contracts theory, leaders can navigate ethical dilemmas with greater flexibility and nuance. As we delve deeper into this chapter, we will explore how these approaches can be applied to develop robust ethical frameworks and guide ethical decision-making processes within organizations.

Metamodern ethics, which blends elements of modernist and postmodernist thinking, offers a robust and adaptable approach to ethical decision-making in contemporary business environments. This framework emphasizes three core principles: flexibility, context-sensitivity, and responsiveness. By incorporating these principles, leaders can develop ethical frameworks that are well-suited to the complexities and dynamics of modern organizations.

Flexibility

Flexibility in ethical frameworks allows organizations to adapt to changing circumstances and emerging challenges. Unlike rigid, rule-based deontological approaches, flexible ethics recognize that ethical dilemmas are often nuanced and multifaceted, requiring a more adaptable response. For example, a company facing an unexpected environmental crisis might need to swiftly re-evaluate its policies and practices to address the immediate issue while considering long-term sustainability. By maintaining flexibility, leaders can make timely decisions that are both practical and morally sound, ensuring that the organization can pivot as needed without compromising its ethical standards.

Context-Sensitivity

Context-sensitivity emphasizes the importance of considering the specific circumstances and cultural contexts in which ethical decisions are made. This principle acknowledges that ethical norms and values can vary significantly across different settings and that a one-size-fits-all approach is often inadequate. For instance, a multinational corporation operating in diverse regions must navigate varying cultural expectations and legal requirements. By being sensitive to these contexts, the company can tailor its practices to respect local customs and regulations while upholding its overarching ethical commitments. This approach not only helps to build trust and credibility but also fosters more effective and harmonious relationships with stakeholders.

Responsiveness

Responsiveness in ethical frameworks entails being proactive and reactive in addressing ethical issues. This principle involves anticipating potential ethical dilemmas and having mechanisms in place to respond swiftly and effectively. For example, a technology firm might establish an ethics committee to oversee the development and deployment of artificial intelligence, ensuring that ethical considerations are integrated from the outset. Additionally, responsiveness requires organizations to be vigilant and agile, capable of adjusting their ethical practices in response to new information, stakeholder feedback, or changing societal norms. This ongoing commitment to ethical responsiveness helps organizations remain relevant and responsible in a rapidly evolving world.

Applying Metamodern Ethics in Business: To operationalize these principles, businesses can adopt several strategies and practices:

Ethical Decision-Making Processes and Models

Implementing structured ethical decision-making processes ensures that flexibility, context-sensitivity, and responsiveness are embedded in organizational practices. One effective model is the Ethical Decision-Making Framework (EDMF), which guides leaders through a series of steps to evaluate ethical dilemmas. The EDMF involves identifying the ethical issue, gathering relevant information, considering the stakeholders involved, exploring alternatives, and making a decision based on a balanced assessment of these factors. This iterative process allows for continuous reflection and adjustment, fostering a flexible and responsive approach to ethics.

Ethics Training and Development

Providing regular ethics training and development opportunities for employees at all levels helps to cultivate a culture of ethical awareness and competence. Training programs should emphasize the importance of flexibility, context-sensitivity, and responsiveness, equipping employees with the skills to navigate complex ethical landscapes. Case studies and simulations can be particularly effective in illustrating how these principles apply in real-world scenarios, reinforcing the practical application of metamodern ethics.

Stakeholder Engagement and Dialogue

Engaging with stakeholders through open and transparent dialogue is crucial for understanding their perspectives and incorporating their values into the organization's ethical framework. Regularly consulting with employees, customers, suppliers, community members, and other stakeholders helps to ensure that the organization remains attuned to evolving ethical expectations and can respond proactively. This ongoing engagement fosters mutual trust and accountability, reinforcing the organization's commitment to ethical excellence.

Ethical Audits and Reviews

Conducting regular ethical audits and reviews helps organizations to assess the effectiveness of their ethical practices and identify areas for improvement. These audits should evaluate how well the principles of flexibility, context-sensitivity, and responsiveness are being integrated into decision-making processes and organizational culture. By continuously monitoring and refining their ethical frameworks, organizations can maintain high ethical standards and adapt to new challenges and opportunities.

In the following sections, we will explore practical applications of these principles through case studies of organizations that have successfully navigated ethical dilemmas using metamodern ethics. These examples will illustrate how flexibility, context-sensitivity, and responsiveness can be effectively implemented to resolve conflicts and guide corporate behavior. Additionally, we will discuss best practices for embedding these principles into organizational culture, ensuring that ethics are not just theoretical but actively practiced and reinforced in daily operations.

By developing ethical frameworks grounded in metamodern principles, leaders can create organizations that are not only resilient and innovative but also ethically sound and socially responsible. This approach provides a comprehensive and adaptable foundation for navigating the ethical complexities of the modern business landscape, fostering trust, and achieving sustainable success.

Incorporating ethical decision-making processes and models is crucial for ensuring that organizational decisions align with the principles of metamodern ethics: flexibility, context-sensitivity, and responsiveness. These models provide structured approaches to navigating complex ethical dilemmas and integrating ethical considerations into everyday business practices.

The Ethical Decision-Making Framework (EDMF)

The Ethical Decision-Making Framework (EDMF) is a comprehensive process that guides leaders through a series of steps to evaluate and address ethical issues systematically. This model helps ensure that decisions are well-considered and ethically sound.

- Identify the Ethical Issue: The first step in the EDMF involves clearly defining the ethical dilemma. This requires recognizing the problem, understanding its ethical implications, and determining who is affected by the issue. For example, a company considering layoffs might identify the ethical issue as balancing financial sustainability with employee well-being.

- Gather Relevant Information: Once the issue is identified, it is essential to collect all pertinent information. This includes factual data, stakeholder perspectives, legal considerations, and any relevant organizational policies. Comprehensive information gathering ensures that the decision-making process is informed and contextual.

- Consider Stakeholders: Evaluating who will be affected by the decision is a critical component of ethical decision-making. Stakeholders can include employees, customers, shareholders, suppliers, and the community. Understanding their interests and how they will be impacted helps in weighing the consequences of different actions.

Explore Alternatives: With the information at hand, the next step is to identify and evaluate possible courses of action. This involves considering multiple solutions and assessing their potential outcomes. Leaders should use ethical principles such as fairness, justice, and harm minimization to guide this evaluation.

- Make a Decision: Based on the analysis of alternatives, leaders can then make a decision that aligns with the organization's ethical values and principles. This decision should aim to balance various interests and achieve the best possible ethical outcome.

- Implement the Decision: Putting the decision into action requires careful planning and execution. Leaders must communicate the decision clearly to all stakeholders and ensure that the implementation process is transparent and accountable.

- Review and Reflect: After the decision has been implemented, it is important to review the outcomes and reflect on the process. This step involves assessing whether the decision achieved the desired ethical outcome and what lessons can be learned for future decision-making.

Virtue Ethics Model

The Virtue Ethics Model focuses on the character and moral virtues of the decision-maker rather than specific actions. This approach emphasizes developing qualities such as honesty, courage, empathy, and integrity. Leaders who embody these virtues are more likely to make ethical decisions consistently.

- Develop Virtues: Organizations can foster virtue ethics by promoting personal development programs that emphasize character building. Workshops, mentorship, and training sessions can help employees cultivate virtues that guide their decision-making.

- Role Models: Leadership should exemplify the virtues they wish to see throughout the organization. By acting as role models, leaders can inspire ethical behavior and create a culture that values moral excellence.

Care Ethics Model

Care ethics emphasizes the importance of relationships, empathy, and caring for others. This model is particularly relevant in contexts where interpersonal relationships and social responsibility are key considerations.

- Empathy and Compassion: Leaders should prioritize understanding and addressing the needs and concerns of stakeholders. This involves active listening, empathetic engagement, and compassionate responses to issues.

- Supportive Policies: Implementing policies that support employee well-being, work-life balance, and community engagement demonstrates a commitment to care ethics. Examples include flexible working hours, comprehensive health benefits, and community outreach programs.

Pragmatic Ethics Model

Pragmatic ethics focuses on practical outcomes and the iterative process of ethical inquiry and adaptation. This model encourages continuous learning and flexibility in addressing ethical issues.

- Iterative Process: Ethical decision-making is viewed as an ongoing process rather than a one-time event. Organizations should be open to revisiting and revising their decisions based on new information and feedback.

- Experimentation and Feedback: Encouraging experimentation with different ethical approaches and gathering feedback from stakeholders helps organizations refine their ethical practices. This iterative approach ensures that ethics remain relevant and responsive to changing circumstances.

Integrative Social Contracts Theory (ISCT)

ISCT combines elements of deontological and non-deontological approaches by emphasizing the role of implicit social agreements in ethical decision-making. This theory posits that ethical norms arise from the agreements and expectations within specific communities or societies.

- Social Contracts: Organizations should consider the implicit social contracts with their stakeholders. This involves understanding and honoring the values and expectations that stakeholders hold.

- Contextual Adaptation: ISCT encourages adapting ethical practices to fit the specific context of different communities or societies. This ensures that ethical standards are culturally sensitive and relevant.

To illustrate these models in action, let's examine a few case studies:

- Environmental Responsibility at Patagonia: Patagonia uses a pragmatic ethics model to continuously improve its environmental practices. By experimenting with new sustainable materials and processes and gathering feedback from customers and environmental groups, Patagonia refines its approach to sustainability, demonstrating flexibility and responsiveness.

- Employee Well-Being at Zappos: Zappos integrates care ethics into its organizational culture by prioritizing employee well-being. The company's policies on flexible working hours, comprehensive health benefits, and a supportive work environment reflect its commitment to empathy and compassion.

- Ethical AI Development at Google: Google's establishment of an AI ethics committee exemplifies the application of the

EDMF. By identifying ethical issues in AI development, gathering relevant information, considering stakeholder impacts, and exploring alternatives, Google aims to make ethical decisions that balance innovation with societal good.

- Community Engagement at Starbucks: Starbucks employs the principles of ISCT by engaging with local communities to understand their values and expectations. This approach ensures that Starbucks' practices are culturally sensitive and aligned with community norms, fostering trust and positive relationships.

Developing ethical frameworks grounded in metamodern principles involves integrating flexibility, context-sensitivity, and responsiveness into decision-making processes. By employing models such as EDMF, virtue ethics, care ethics, pragmatic ethics, and ISCT, organizations can navigate complex ethical landscapes and make decisions that are both practical and morally sound. These approaches ensure that ethics are deeply embedded in organizational practices, fostering a culture of integrity and social responsibility.

To understand how metamodern ethical frameworks can be applied in real-world business scenarios, we will explore several case studies that highlight ethical dilemmas and their resolutions. These examples illustrate how principles like flexibility, context-sensitivity, and responsiveness can guide organizations in navigating complex ethical challenges.

Patagonia, an outdoor apparel company, faced the challenge of balancing its commitment to environmental sustainability with the need to remain profitable. The company identified that the production of its clothing had a significant environmental impact, including carbon emissions and waste. Patagonia adopted a pragmatic ethics approach, continuously experimenting with sustainable materials and production processes. The company implemented the Ethical Decision-Making Framework (EDMF) to guide its efforts by recognizing the environmental impact of its operations, conducting life cycle assessments of its products to understand their environmental footprint, and engaging with environmental organizations, customers, and employees to gather diverse perspectives. They investigated sustainable materials such as recycled polyester and organic cotton and decided to commit to using 100% recycled polyester in its products while launching the "Worn Wear" program to encourage product reuse and repair. By integrating sustainable practices across the supply chain and promoting the "Worn Wear" program to customers, Patagonia continuously assessed the impact of these initiatives and sought further improvements. This approach allowed Patagonia to reduce its environmental impact while maintaining profitability, demonstrating flexibility and responsiveness to both ethical and business imperatives.

Zappos, an online shoe and clothing retailer, wanted to enhance employee well-being and create a supportive work environment. The challenge was to balance this goal with the demands of a fast-paced e-commerce business. Zappos applied the care ethics model, emphasizing empathy and compassion in its policies. The company encouraged leaders and employees to cultivate empathy and compassion, with leadership demonstrating a commitment to employee well-being through transparent and supportive practices. Implementing flexible working hours and comprehensive health benefits supported work-life balance, and creating a positive workplace culture through initiatives like the "Culture Book," which shares employee stories and feedback, further reinforced this approach. By prioritizing employee well-being, Zappos fostered a loyal and motivated workforce, enhancing overall productivity and customer satisfaction.

Google faced ethical concerns regarding the development and deployment of artificial intelligence (AI), including issues such as data privacy, algorithmic bias, and the potential for misuse of AI technologies. Google established an AI ethics committee and used the EDMF to guide its decisions by recognizing the potential ethical implications of AI technologies, consulting with experts in ethics, law, and technology to understand the risks and benefits, and engaging with users, policymakers, and civil society organizations to gather input on ethical concerns. Evaluating different approaches to AI development, including transparency in AI algorithms and bias mitigation techniques, led to the implementation of guidelines for ethical AI development such as fairness, accountability, and transparency. Integrating these guidelines into AI projects and conducting regular audits to ensure compliance, Google continuously monitored the ethical impact of AI technologies and updated policies as needed. This approach allowed Google to address ethical concerns proactively and build trust with stakeholders, ensuring responsible AI development.

Starbucks aimed to engage with local communities to ensure its business practices were culturally sensitive and aligned with community values. The challenge was to balance global brand consistency with local customization. Starbucks applied Integrative Social Contracts Theory (ISCT) to navigate this dilemma by understanding the implicit social contracts with local communities by engaging with community leaders and customers. Tailoring store designs, product offerings, and community programs to reflect local cultures and preferences, Starbucks developed community engagement initiatives such as "Community Stores," which partner with local organizations to support social and economic development. Regularly assessing the impact of these initiatives and adjusting strategies based on community feedback, Starbucks respected and integrated local values into its operations, strengthening its relationships with communities and enhancing its brand reputation.

These case studies illustrate how organizations can apply metamodern ethical principles to address complex dilemmas effectively. By leveraging flexibility, context-sensitivity, and responsiveness, businesses can develop ethical frameworks that guide decision-making and foster trust with stakeholders. These practical applications demonstrate the value of integrating ethics into organizational culture, ensuring that companies not only achieve business success but also uphold their social and ethical responsibilities.

Embedding ethics in organizational culture is essential for ensuring that ethical principles are not merely theoretical but actively practiced and reinforced daily. This requires a multifaceted approach that integrates ethical considerations into every aspect of the organization's operations and decision-making processes.

One effective practice is to establish a clear and comprehensive code of ethics that outlines the organization's core values and ethical standards. This document should be communicated to all employees, from entry-level staff to top executives, and integrated into training programs to ensure everyone understands and commits to these principles. Regular workshops and seminars can reinforce this knowledge, providing opportunities for employees to discuss ethical dilemmas and explore how to apply the organization's values in various situations.

Leadership plays a crucial role in setting the tone for an ethical culture. Leaders must model ethical behavior consistently, demonstrating a commitment to the organization's values in their actions and decisions. This includes making transparent and fair decisions, acknowledging and rectifying mistakes, and holding themselves and others accountable for unethical behavior. When employees see their leaders acting with integrity, they are more likely to follow suit, creating a culture of trust and respect.

Open and transparent communication is another cornerstone of an ethical culture. Organizations should encourage open dialogue about ethical issues, providing channels for employees to voice concerns or report unethical behavior without fear of retaliation. Implementing a robust whistleblower policy and ensuring that employees are aware of and feel safe using these reporting mechanisms is critical. Regularly communicating the outcomes of ethical reviews and the steps taken to address any issues reinforces the organization's commitment to ethics and accountability.

Incorporating ethical considerations into performance evaluations and reward systems can further embed ethics in organizational culture. By recognizing and rewarding employees who demonstrate ethical behavior and contribute to the organization's ethical goals, companies can reinforce the importance of these values. Conversely, unethical behavior should be addressed promptly and appropriately, ensuring that ethical standards are upheld consistently.

Engaging stakeholders in ethical discussions and decision-making processes can also strengthen an organization's ethical culture. This includes soliciting input from employees, customers, suppliers, and the community on ethical issues and incorporating their feedback into the organization's policies and practices. By involving stakeholders in these discussions, organizations can build a broader consensus on ethical standards and enhance their credibility and trustworthiness.

Ongoing ethical audits and assessments are essential for maintaining and improving ethical standards within an organization. These reviews should evaluate the effectiveness of existing ethical policies and practices, identify areas for improvement, and ensure that the organization adapts to new ethical challenges as they arise. Regularly updating the code of ethics and other related documents to reflect these findings helps keep the organization's ethical framework relevant and robust.

By embedding ethics into every facet of the organization, businesses can create a culture that prioritizes integrity, accountability, and social responsibility. This not only enhances the organization's reputation and trustworthiness but also contributes to long-term success by fostering a loyal and motivated workforce, attracting ethical partners and customers, and minimizing the risks associated with unethical behavior.

Incorporating ethics in organizational culture involves a comprehensive approach that integrates ethical principles into leadership practices, communication strategies, performance evaluations, stakeholder engagement, and ongoing assessments. By committing to these best practices, organizations can ensure that their ethical values are lived and practiced daily, creating a sustainable and responsible business environment.

Chapter 4: New Forms of Power and Resistance

As organizations continue to evolve, so too do the dynamics of power within them. Traditional power structures, characterized by rigid hierarchies and top-down authority, are increasingly being challenged by more flexible and decentralized models. This shift reflects broader changes in society and the workforce, where empowerment, inclusion, and collaboration are becoming essential elements of effective leadership.

In this chapter, we will examine conventional power dynamics in organizations, exploring how traditional hierarchies have functioned and why they are often no longer suitable in today's complex and fast-paced business environment. These traditional structures, while providing clear lines of authority and decision-making, often stifle innovation, limit employee engagement, and create barriers to effective communication.

Emerging alternative power structures offer a more adaptable approach. These models emphasize distributed leadership, where power is shared among team members rather than concentrated at the top. This approach allows for more agile decision-making and fosters a culture of empowerment and accountability. We will explore various forms of these alternative structures, from flat organizations to networked teams, and discuss how they can lead to greater innovation and resilience.

Understanding resistance in a post-postmodern context is crucial for navigating these new power dynamics. Resistance is not merely a barrier to be overcome but a natural and potentially beneficial response to change. By understanding the roots and expressions of resistance, leaders can develop strategies to manage it constructively. Embracing resistance can lead to more robust decision-making processes, as it often highlights areas of concern that need to be addressed. We will delve into the various modes of resistance and provide strategies for managing and integrating them into the organizational change process.

Empowerment and inclusion are fundamental to fostering environments where new power dynamics can thrive. By empowering employees and promoting inclusive practices, organizations can tap into a wider range of perspectives and talents, driving innovation and growth. Methods for fostering such environments will be discussed, with practical examples and case studies illustrating successful implementations.

Through these case studies, we will examine organizations that have successfully implemented new power dynamics, highlighting the challenges they faced and the strategies they used to overcome them. These examples will provide valuable insights into how power can be redefined and distributed in ways that enhance organizational effectiveness and employee satisfaction.

As we explore these themes, this chapter will offer a comprehensive understanding of how new forms of power and resistance can be harnessed to create more dynamic, inclusive, and resilient organizations. By challenging traditional power structures and embracing alternative models, leaders can foster a culture of empowerment and innovation, positioning their organizations for success in the modern business landscape.

Traditional power structures in organizations have long been characterized by rigid hierarchies, where authority and decision-making flow from the top down. These conventional models, often depicted as pyramids, place senior executives and managers at the apex, with layers of middle management beneath, and frontline employees at the base. This structure has been the cornerstone of organizational design for decades, providing clear lines of authority and a straightforward chain of command.

In such hierarchies, power is concentrated in the hands of a few individuals who make the key decisions, set the strategic direction, and control resources. This centralization of power ensures that decisions are consistent and aligned with the organization's overarching goals. It also facilitates accountability, as it is clear who is responsible for outcomes. However, this model has significant limitations, especially in the context of today's fast-paced, complex, and dynamic business environment.

One major drawback of traditional hierarchical structures is their inherent inflexibility. Decision-making in these organizations can be slow, as approval must often travel through multiple layers of management. This can hinder responsiveness and adaptability, critical components for success in the modern market where conditions change rapidly, and timely decisions are crucial. Hierarchies can also create bottlenecks, as decision-making authority is concentrated at the top, limiting the input and innovation from lower levels of the organization.

Rigid hierarchies can stifle creativity and innovation. Employees at lower levels may feel disempowered or disengaged, believing that their ideas and contributions are undervalued or ignored. This can lead to a lack of motivation and a decrease in overall productivity. The top-down approach to decision-making often means that those who are closest to the work and understand it best—frontline employees—are not involved in shaping the solutions to problems they face daily.

The concentration of power in traditional hierarchies also tends to perpetuate inequality and limit diversity. When decision-making is confined to a small, often homogenous group at the top, the organization may lack diverse perspectives and fail to address the needs and ideas of a broader workforce. This can result in policies and strategies that do not fully leverage the potential of all employees, particularly those from different backgrounds and experiences.

Traditional power structures can create a culture of dependency, where employees rely heavily on their managers for direction and approval. This can undermine individual initiative and the development of leadership skills at all levels. It can also lead to a lack of ownership and accountability, as employees may feel less responsible for outcomes that they had little influence over.

In contrast to these conventional models, alternative power structures are emerging that seek to address these limitations. These new models emphasize distributed leadership, where power is shared among team members, and decisions are made collaboratively. This approach can enhance agility, foster innovation, and create a more inclusive and engaged workforce.

Organizations like Valve Corporation, with its flat organizational structure, illustrate how power can be decentralized. At Valve, there are no formal job titles or hierarchies; employees are free to take on roles and projects that align with their interests and expertise. This structure empowers employees to make decisions and take ownership of their work, leading to higher levels of engagement and innovation.

Similarly, companies like W.L. Gore & Associates have adopted lattice structures that promote fluid communication and collaboration across the organization. In these models, leadership emerges organically based on expertise and the ability to influence rather than formal titles. This fosters a culture of mutual respect and continuous learning, as employees are encouraged to share their knowledge and contribute to the organization's success.

While traditional power structures have provided a foundation for organizational design, their limitations are increasingly apparent in today's dynamic business environment. Challenging these conventional models by adopting more flexible and distributed power structures can lead to greater innovation, inclusivity, and responsiveness. By examining and understanding these alternative approaches, organizations can better navigate the complexities of the modern market and harness the full potential of their workforce.

The emergence of alternative power structures in organizations represents a significant shift away from traditional hierarchical models. These new structures are designed to address the limitations of rigid hierarchies by promoting flexibility, collaboration, and empowerment. As businesses face increasingly complex and dynamic environments, the need for more adaptive and inclusive power dynamics has become evident. Here, we delve deeper into various alternative power structures and their impact on organizational effectiveness.

One prominent example of alternative power structures is the flat organization. Flat organizations reduce or eliminate hierarchical layers, promoting a more egalitarian approach to management. In these structures, all employees have equal opportunity to contribute ideas and participate in decision-making processes. This model fosters a culture of transparency and open communication, as employees are encouraged to share their perspectives without the constraints of hierarchical barriers. Valve Corporation is a well-known proponent of this approach. At Valve, there are no formal job titles or managerial hierarchies, allowing employees to self-organize around projects that interest them. This autonomy has led to high levels of creativity and innovation, as employees feel empowered to take initiative and pursue their passions.

Another example is the networked organization, which emphasizes interconnectedness and collaboration across traditional boundaries. Networked organizations leverage digital tools and technologies to facilitate seamless communication and coordination among teams, regardless of their physical location. This structure is particularly effective in fostering agility and responsiveness, as teams can quickly form, adapt, and disband based on the needs of the organization. For instance, companies like IBM have adopted networked structures to enhance their global operations. By utilizing collaborative platforms and cloud-based technologies, IBM enables its employees to work together effectively across different regions and time zones, driving innovation and improving customer service.

Holacracy is another innovative power structure that has gained traction in recent years. Holacracy replaces traditional hierarchies with a system of self-managing teams called circles. Each circle operates autonomously, with clearly defined roles and responsibilities that are regularly updated through structured governance processes. This approach encourages a high degree of accountability and transparency, as decisions are made collectively and roles are distributed based on expertise rather than formal titles. Zappos, an online shoe and clothing retailer, implemented Holacracy to foster a more flexible and adaptive organizational culture. By empowering employees to take ownership of their work and make decisions within their circles, Zappos has been able to maintain a high level of employee engagement and innovation.

The rise of the agile organization is another example of an alternative power structure that prioritizes flexibility and customer-centricity. Agile organizations adopt iterative processes and cross-functional teams to deliver value quickly and efficiently. This approach is particularly popular in the technology sector, where companies need to rapidly respond to changing market demands and technological advancements. Spotify, the music streaming giant, exemplifies the agile organization with its use of "squads," "tribes," and "guilds." Squads are small, cross-functional teams that operate autonomously, while tribes are collections of squads that work on related areas. Guilds, on the other hand, are communities of interest that span across squads and tribes, allowing employees to share knowledge and best practices. This structure enables Spotify to innovate continuously and respond quickly to user feedback and technological changes.

Sociocracy, another alternative power structure, integrates principles of democracy and consent-based decision-making into organizational governance. In a sociocratic organization, decisions are made through a process of consent, where all members must agree that a proposal is acceptable for it to move forward. This approach ensures that all voices are heard and that decisions reflect the collective wisdom of the group. Organizations like Buurtzorg, a Dutch home-care provider, have successfully implemented sociocracy to create a more inclusive and participatory work environment. Buurtzorg's self-managing teams of nurses make decisions collaboratively, leading to high levels of employee satisfaction and improved patient care.

The rise of hybrid organizational models also illustrates the blending of traditional and alternative power structures. Hybrid models combine elements of hierarchy with more flexible and decentralized approaches, allowing organizations to benefit from the stability of traditional structures while gaining the agility of alternative models. For example, Haier, a global appliance manufacturer, has adopted the Rendanheyi model, which transforms the company into a network of micro-enterprises. Each micro-enterprise operates with a high degree of autonomy, making decisions and managing resources independently while being aligned with the overall strategic goals of the organization. This hybrid approach enables Haier to remain innovative and responsive while maintaining strategic coherence.

The emergence of alternative power structures reflects a broader trend towards more adaptive, inclusive, and empowering organizational models. By moving away from rigid hierarchies and embracing flat organizations, networked structures, Holacracy, agile frameworks, sociocracy, and hybrid models, businesses can better navigate the complexities of the modern market. These alternative power structures promote collaboration, innovation, and employee engagement, positioning organizations for long-term success in a rapidly changing world. As we continue to explore new forms of power and resistance, it becomes clear that flexibility and inclusivity are key to creating resilient and dynamic organizations.

In the contemporary business environment, resistance to change is a common phenomenon that can manifest in various forms. Understanding resistance in a post-postmodern context requires recognizing it not as a mere obstacle to be overcome but as a potentially valuable feedback mechanism that can enhance decision-making and organizational development. Resistance can highlight areas of concern, reveal hidden issues, and provide insights that lead to more robust and inclusive strategies.

One mode of resistance is overt resistance, which includes clear and visible actions such as strikes, protests, or open dissent. These actions are often organized by employees or other stakeholders who feel that their concerns are not being adequately addressed. For example, employees might stage a walkout to protest unfair labor practices or inadequate working conditions. Overt resistance signals a strong level of dissatisfaction and a need for immediate attention and dialogue from leadership.

Another mode is covert resistance, which involves more subtle and less visible actions. This can include passive-aggressive behaviors, reduced productivity, or increased absenteeism. Employees engaging in covert resistance might comply with the letter of new policies while undermining their spirit. This type of resistance can be harder to detect and address because it operates below the surface, yet it can significantly impact organizational morale and effectiveness over time.

Symbolic resistance is another important form to consider, where stakeholders use symbols, language, or cultural references to express their opposition. This could involve the use of social media hashtags, cultural artifacts, or other symbolic acts that convey resistance without direct confrontation. For instance, employees might wear specific colors or symbols to silently protest a policy or decision. Understanding the cultural and symbolic context of such resistance can help leaders grasp the deeper values and concerns driving the opposition.

Constructive resistance represents a proactive and positive form of opposition. Individuals or groups who engage in constructive resistance offer alternative solutions, provide critical feedback, and engage in dialogue to improve outcomes. This form of resistance can be highly beneficial as it channels opposition into productive and collaborative efforts. Encouraging constructive resistance involves creating safe spaces for dialogue, actively soliciting feedback, and demonstrating a willingness to adapt and learn from dissenting voices.

Ideological resistance occurs when stakeholders oppose changes based on deeply held beliefs or values. This type of resistance is often rooted in cultural, ethical, or ideological differences and can be particularly challenging to address. For example, a company implementing artificial intelligence might face resistance from employees who have ethical concerns about privacy and job displacement. Addressing ideological resistance requires engaging with the underlying values and working to find common ground or acceptable compromises.

Understanding these various modes of resistance in a post-postmodern context involves recognizing the complexity and multifaceted nature of opposition. It requires leaders to move beyond viewing resistance as a threat and instead see it as an opportunity for engagement and growth. By adopting a more nuanced approach, leaders can develop strategies to manage and embrace resistance constructively.

Dialogue and Engagement are crucial strategies for managing resistance. Leaders should create open channels of communication where employees feel safe expressing their concerns. Regular town hall meetings, focus groups, and anonymous feedback mechanisms can help surface issues early and allow for collaborative problem-solving. For example, a company facing resistance to a new digital tool might hold workshops to understand employees' concerns and co-create solutions that address their needs while achieving organizational goals.

Transparency and Inclusion are also key. Being transparent about the reasons for change and involving employees in the decision-making process can reduce resistance. When people understand the rationale behind changes and have a say in how they are implemented, they are more likely to support them. This inclusive approach not only mitigates resistance but also leverages the collective intelligence of the organization.

Empathy and Support are essential for addressing the emotional and psychological aspects of resistance. Change can be unsettling, and acknowledging the fears and anxieties that come with it is important. Providing support through counseling, training, and clear communication can help ease the transition and build trust. For instance, when a company undergoes a major restructuring, offering career coaching and professional development opportunities can help employees navigate the change more confidently.

Understanding resistance in a post-postmodern context involves recognizing its various forms and the valuable insights it can provide. By embracing resistance as a source of feedback and potential improvement, leaders can foster a more inclusive and adaptive organizational culture. Strategies such as dialogue and engagement, transparency and inclusion, and empathy and support are key to managing and harnessing resistance constructively, ultimately leading to more resilient and innovative organizations.

Strategies for Managing and Embracing Resistance Constructively

Managing and embracing resistance constructively is essential for fostering a resilient and innovative organizational culture. By viewing resistance as a valuable source of feedback and potential improvement, leaders can transform opposition into opportunities for growth. Here are several strategies to effectively manage and embrace resistance:

Dialogue and Engagement are critical for understanding the concerns underlying resistance. Leaders should establish open channels of communication where employees feel safe to express their views. Regular town hall meetings, focus groups, and anonymous surveys can provide platforms for employees to voice their opinions. For example, a company introducing a new technology might hold workshops to gather employee feedback, discuss potential challenges, and collaboratively develop solutions. This approach not only surfaces issues early but also promotes a sense of ownership and involvement among employees.

Transparency and Inclusion are fundamental in reducing resistance. When leaders are transparent about the reasons for change and include employees in the decision-making process, it fosters trust and cooperation. Clearly explaining the rationale behind changes and how they align with the organization's goals helps employees understand the bigger picture. Involving employees in planning and implementation phases ensures that their insights and concerns are considered, making them more likely to support the changes. For instance, a company restructuring its operations could form cross-functional teams to design the new structure, ensuring that diverse perspectives are represented.

Empathy and Support address the emotional and psychological aspects of resistance. Change can be unsettling, and acknowledging employees' fears and anxieties is crucial. Leaders should show empathy by listening to employees' concerns and providing reassurance. Support mechanisms such as counseling services, training programs, and clear communication can help ease the transition. For example, during a major organizational change, offering professional development opportunities and career coaching can help employees adapt and build new skills, reducing their anxiety and resistance.

Fostering a Culture of Feedback encourages continuous improvement and openness. Creating an environment where feedback is regularly sought and valued can turn resistance into constructive dialogue. Leaders should actively solicit feedback on changes and show that they are willing to adjust plans based on employee input. This iterative approach ensures that changes are refined and improved over time. For example, after implementing a new process, a company might hold follow-up meetings to gather feedback and make necessary adjustments, demonstrating a commitment to listening and evolving.

Recognizing and Rewarding Constructive Resistance can turn opposition into a positive force. When employees offer thoughtful critiques or alternative solutions, recognizing and rewarding their contributions can encourage more constructive engagement. This could involve acknowledging their input in meetings, offering formal recognition, or providing incentives for innovative ideas. By valuing constructive resistance, leaders signal that they welcome diverse perspectives and are committed to continuous improvement.

Leveraging Champions and Influencers within the organization can help manage resistance. Identifying and engaging employees who are influential and respected by their peers can facilitate smoother transitions. These champions can help communicate the benefits of changes, address concerns, and model positive behaviors. For instance, a company implementing a new software system might train a group of early adopters who can support their colleagues and advocate for the new system.

Implementing Pilot Programs and Phased Rollouts can mitigate resistance by allowing for gradual adjustment. Pilot programs enable organizations to test changes on a smaller scale, gather feedback, and make improvements before wider implementation. Phased rollouts can help manage the pace of change, allowing employees time to adapt. For example, a company introducing a new performance management system might start with a pilot in one department, refine the approach based on feedback, and then roll it out gradually across the organization.

Training and Development Programs equip employees with the skills and knowledge needed to adapt to changes. Comprehensive training programs can reduce resistance by building confidence and competence. Providing ongoing learning opportunities ensures that employees feel prepared and supported. For instance, during a digital transformation, offering extensive training on new technologies and processes can help employees feel more comfortable and capable, reducing their resistance.

Managing and embracing resistance constructively involves a combination of dialogue, transparency, empathy, and support. By fostering a culture of feedback, recognizing constructive resistance, leveraging champions, implementing pilot programs, and providing training, leaders can turn opposition into opportunities for growth. These strategies not only help manage resistance effectively but also build a more resilient and innovative organizational culture, ultimately leading to sustainable success in a dynamic business environment.

Empowering employees and fostering an inclusive environment are essential for creating a dynamic and innovative organization. Empowerment involves giving employees the autonomy, resources, and support they need to make decisions and take initiative. Inclusion ensures that all employees, regardless of their background, have equal opportunities to contribute and succeed. Together, these elements create a culture where everyone feels valued, respected, and motivated to perform at their best.

One effective method for fostering empowerment and inclusion is to establish a clear and compelling vision that emphasizes these values. Communicating this vision consistently helps align the organization's goals with the principles of empowerment and inclusion. Leaders play a crucial role in modeling these behaviors, demonstrating a commitment to diversity and inclusion in their actions and decisions. When employees see leaders championing these values, they are more likely to embrace and practice them as well.

Creating opportunities for employees to participate in decision-making processes is another vital approach. This can be achieved through regular town hall meetings, focus groups, and suggestion programs where employees can voice their ideas and concerns. By involving employees in shaping policies and initiatives, organizations show that they value diverse perspectives and are open to input from all levels. This not only enhances engagement but also leads to better decision-making as a wider range of viewpoints is considered.

Training and development programs focused on diversity, equity, and inclusion (DEI) are essential for fostering an inclusive environment. These programs should educate employees about the importance of inclusion, unconscious bias, and cultural competence. Providing ongoing learning opportunities ensures that employees continue to develop their understanding and skills in these areas. For instance, workshops and seminars can help employees recognize and address their biases, while mentoring programs can support underrepresented groups in their career development.

Establishing Employee Resource Groups (ERGs) can also significantly enhance inclusion. ERGs are voluntary, employee-led groups that provide support and networking opportunities for members of diverse communities within the organization. These groups can offer a platform for discussing common challenges, sharing experiences, and advocating for necessary changes. By supporting ERGs, organizations can foster a sense of belonging and community, helping employees feel more connected and engaged.

Implementing inclusive hiring and promotion practices is crucial for ensuring that all employees have equal opportunities to succeed. This involves reviewing and refining recruitment processes to eliminate bias, setting diversity targets, and ensuring that job descriptions and criteria are inclusive. Additionally, providing training for hiring managers on inclusive practices can help create a more diverse workforce. Transparent and equitable promotion processes, where criteria are clearly defined and opportunities are accessible to all, further reinforce a commitment to inclusion.

Flexible work arrangements are another important aspect of fostering an inclusive environment. Recognizing that employees have diverse needs and responsibilities, offering options such as remote work, flexible hours, and job sharing can help accommodate different lifestyles and enhance work-life balance. This flexibility not only supports employee well-being but also attracts a wider range of talent to the organization.

Regularly measuring and reporting on diversity and inclusion metrics is essential for tracking progress and holding the organization accountable. Surveys, audits, and performance reviews focused on DEI can provide valuable insights into how well the organization is doing and where improvements are needed. Sharing these findings transparently with employees demonstrates a commitment to continuous improvement and fosters trust.

Creating a culture of recognition and celebration of diversity helps reinforce the value of inclusion. Celebrating cultural events, acknowledging diverse holidays, and recognizing the contributions of employees from different backgrounds can create a more welcoming and inclusive atmosphere. These celebrations not only highlight the organization's commitment to diversity but also educate employees about different cultures and perspectives.

Providing safe spaces for open dialogue and addressing issues related to discrimination and harassment promptly and effectively is crucial. Establishing clear policies and procedures for reporting and addressing grievances ensures that employees feel safe and supported. Offering confidential reporting channels and ensuring that complaints are handled with sensitivity and fairness helps build trust and a sense of security.

Fostering an inclusive environment and empowering employees involves a multifaceted approach that integrates clear vision and leadership, participatory decision-making, comprehensive DEI training, support for ERGs, inclusive hiring practices, flexible work arrangements, regular measurement and accountability, cultural recognition, and safe spaces for dialogue. By committing to these methods, organizations can create a culture where all employees feel valued, respected, and motivated to contribute their best, driving innovation and success in a diverse and dynamic business landscape.

Examining how various organizations have successfully implemented new power dynamics provides valuable insights into the practical applications of empowerment and inclusion. These case studies illustrate the diverse ways in which companies can transform their organizational structures to foster more dynamic, inclusive, and resilient environments.

Morning Star Company

The Morning Star Company, a major player in the tomato processing industry, operates with a self-management philosophy. Morning Star has no formal job titles or managers; instead, employees, referred to as "colleagues," are empowered to take full responsibility for their roles. Each colleague negotiates responsibilities with peers and sets personal mission statements that align with the company's objectives. This model encourages initiative, accountability, and collaboration, leading to high employee satisfaction and operational efficiency. Morning Star's success demonstrates the potential of eliminating traditional hierarchies in favor of a self-management approach.

Semco Partners

Semco Partners, a Brazilian company known for its radical approach to management, has implemented a participatory management style that significantly departs from traditional power structures. Under the leadership of Ricardo Semler, Semco adopted practices such as open financials, flexible work hours, and employee profit-sharing. Employees have significant autonomy, including the power to set their own salaries and vote on major business decisions. This inclusive and democratic approach has led to increased productivity, innovation, and employee engagement, showcasing the benefits of distributing power and fostering a participative culture.

IDEO

IDEO, a global design and consulting firm, uses a flat and flexible organizational structure to foster creativity and innovation. The company is known for its "design thinking" approach, which emphasizes empathy, experimentation, and collaboration. Teams at IDEO are self-organized around projects, with leaders emerging based on the needs of each project rather than hierarchical titles. This fluid structure allows IDEO to adapt quickly to client needs and market changes, driving continuous innovation. IDEO's success in creating groundbreaking products and services highlights the effectiveness of a flat organizational model that empowers teams.

Netflix

Netflix has cultivated a culture of freedom and responsibility that empowers employees at all levels. The company's approach includes minimal formal policies and a high level of trust in employees to act in the best interests of the organization. For instance, Netflix's "unlimited vacation" policy allows employees to take as much time off as they need, as long as their work is completed effectively. Decision-making is decentralized, with employees encouraged to make decisions and take risks. This empowerment fosters innovation and agility, enabling Netflix to remain a leader in the competitive streaming industry.

Patagonia

Patagonia, the outdoor apparel company, has implemented an empowerment strategy centered on environmental responsibility and employee engagement. The company operates with a decentralized structure that allows employees to take initiative in sustainability efforts and product innovation. Patagonia encourages its employees to participate in environmental activism and grants them time off to volunteer for causes they are passionate about. This empowerment, combined with a strong commitment to environmental ethics, has resulted in a loyal and motivated workforce and a brand renowned for its integrity and innovation.

Zingerman's Community of Businesses

Zingerman's Community of Businesses, based in Ann Arbor, Michigan, is a collection of food-related enterprises that operate with a collaborative and inclusive model. Each business within the community is run semi-autonomously, with shared ownership and decision-making responsibilities among employees. Zingerman's places a strong emphasis on training, transparency, and open-book management, where financial information is shared with all employees. This inclusive approach has fostered a strong sense of ownership and accountability, leading to high levels of employee engagement and customer satisfaction.

Nucor Corporation

Nucor Corporation, a leading steel production company, employs a decentralized management structure that empowers employees at all levels. Each plant operates as an independent profit center, with teams given significant autonomy to manage operations and make decisions. Nucor's culture emphasizes performance-based rewards, with employees receiving bonuses tied to the success of their team and the company as a whole. This approach has led to high productivity, innovation, and a strong alignment between employee and organizational goals.

These case studies demonstrate that various forms of new power dynamics can be successfully implemented across different industries and organizational contexts. Whether through self-management, participatory management, flat structures, or decentralized decision-making, these organizations have shown that empowering employees and fostering inclusive environments lead to enhanced innovation, resilience, and overall performance. By embracing these new power dynamics, companies can better navigate the complexities of the modern business landscape and achieve sustainable success.

Chapter 5: The Integration of Play and Creativity

As businesses strive to remain competitive and innovative, the integration of play and creativity into the workplace has emerged as a powerful strategy. This chapter explores how fostering an environment that encourages play and creativity can lead to increased innovation, employee satisfaction, and overall organizational success.

Historically, the work ethic has been deeply rooted in the values of diligence, discipline, and productivity, often viewing play and leisure as distractions. The Protestant work ethic, for instance, emphasized hard work, frugality, and the deferment of pleasure. However, as the nature of work evolves in the 21st century, there is a growing recognition that play is not antithetical to productivity. Instead, it is an essential component of a healthy and innovative work environment.

Integrating play into professional settings offers numerous benefits. Playful activities can reduce stress, enhance problem-solving abilities, and foster better team dynamics. It encourages employees to experiment, take risks, and think outside the box, all of which are critical for innovation. Companies like Google and LEGO have successfully integrated play into their cultures, creating environments where creativity flourishes and groundbreaking ideas emerge.

Fostering creativity involves more than just occasional team-building activities or creative brainstorming sessions. It requires a deliberate and sustained effort to cultivate a culture that values and nurtures creativity. Techniques for encouraging creativity include providing employees with the autonomy to explore new ideas, offering diverse and stimulating work environments, and encouraging cross-functional collaboration. Additionally, organizations can implement programs that celebrate and reward creative achievements, thereby reinforcing the importance of innovation.

Practical strategies for promoting play and creativity at work can take many forms. Activities and exercises designed to stimulate the imagination and foster a sense of playfulness can be integrated into daily routines. These might include creativity workshops, hackathons, and design thinking sessions. Moreover, creating physical spaces that inspire creativity, such as open-plan offices, relaxation areas, and innovation labs, can make a significant difference.

Measuring the impact of playful and creative initiatives is crucial to understanding their effectiveness and justifying their implementation. Organizations can use a variety of metrics to assess the benefits, such as employee engagement surveys, productivity measures, and innovation output. By analyzing these metrics, companies can refine their approaches to fostering play and creativity, ensuring that these initiatives contribute meaningfully to their overall goals.

This chapter will delve into the historical perspective on work ethic and play, highlighting the shift towards integrating play into the workplace. It will discuss the benefits of such integration, providing evidence and examples from leading organizations. Techniques for fostering creativity and practical strategies for promoting play at work will be explored in detail, along with methods for measuring their impact. By understanding and implementing these concepts, leaders can create environments that not only enhance employee well-being but also drive sustained innovation and success.

Play is an often underappreciated but highly effective tool in the modern workplace. While traditionally, the work ethic has emphasized seriousness and productivity, recent shifts in understanding highlight the significant benefits of integrating play into professional settings. Play is not merely a break from work; it is a critical component that fosters creativity, innovation, and employee well-being.

Historically, the notion of work was separated from play, rooted in the Protestant work ethic that emphasized hard work, discipline, and frugality. This ethic shaped the industrial era, where productivity and efficiency were paramount, and any form of play was seen as counterproductive. However, as we move further into the 21st century, the lines between work and play are increasingly blurred, reflecting a deeper understanding of human psychology and organizational behavior.

The concept of the Protestant work ethic, popularized by sociologist Max Weber in his seminal work "The Protestant Ethic and the Spirit of Capitalism," has significantly influenced Western attitudes towards work and play. This ethic, rooted in the teachings of Protestant reformers like Martin Luther and John Calvin, emphasized hard work, frugality, and a sense of duty as moral imperatives. According to this view, diligent labor was seen as a form of worship and a means of achieving personal salvation, while idleness and play were often regarded with suspicion and disapproval. This religious and moral framework laid the foundation for a culture that prioritized productivity and efficiency over leisure and enjoyment.

During the Industrial Revolution in the 18th and 19th centuries, the emphasis on productivity and discipline became even more pronounced. The rise of factories and mechanized production demanded regimented work schedules and strict adherence to routines. Workers were expected to perform repetitive tasks for long hours under close supervision, with little room for creativity or relaxation. The factory system reinforced the notion that play and leisure were distractions from the serious business of work. This era saw the solidification of the work-play dichotomy, with clear boundaries drawn between time allocated for labor and time for rest.

In the early 20th century, the advent of scientific management, also known as Taylorism, further entrenched these attitudes.

Pioneered by Frederick Winslow Taylor, this approach sought to optimize labor productivity through time-and-motion studies and standardized work processes. Taylorism emphasized efficiency, control, and the elimination of waste, viewing workers as components in a larger machine. In this context, play had no place in the workplace, as it was seen as counterproductive to the goals of maximizing output and minimizing costs.

Despite these dominant trends, the late 20th century witnessed a gradual shift in attitudes towards work and play. The rise of human relations and organizational behavior theories highlighted the importance of employee well-being, motivation, and job satisfaction. Researchers like Elton Mayo, Abraham Maslow, and Douglas McGregor argued that recognizing and addressing the social and psychological needs of workers could enhance productivity and overall organizational effectiveness. This shift laid the groundwork for a more holistic understanding of work, which began to acknowledge the value of integrating play and creativity into the workplace.

The information age and the growth of the knowledge economy in the late 20th and early 21st centuries further transformed the landscape of work. In knowledge-based industries, where innovation and creativity are key drivers of success, the rigid separation between work and play became increasingly untenable. Companies like Google, Apple, and IDEO pioneered new workplace cultures that embraced flexibility, autonomy, and play as essential components of their business strategies. These organizations recognized that fostering a playful and creative environment could spur innovation, attract top talent, and enhance employee engagement.

Today, the integration of play into the workplace reflects a broader recognition of its multifaceted benefits. Play reduces stress, enhances problem-solving abilities, and fosters better team dynamics. It encourages employees to experiment, take risks, and think outside the box, all of which are critical for innovation. Moreover, a playful work environment can improve job satisfaction and employee retention, contributing to a more positive organizational culture.

The benefits of integrating play into the workplace are manifold. Play reduces stress, a significant factor in enhancing overall employee well-being. When employees are less stressed, they are more likely to be engaged, productive, and committed to their work. Play also enhances problem-solving skills and cognitive flexibility. Engaging in playful activities stimulates different parts of the brain, encouraging innovative thinking and allowing employees to approach problems from new angles.

Play fosters better team dynamics. Shared playful experiences build trust, improve communication, and strengthen relationships among team members. Activities such as team-building exercises, games, and informal gatherings help break down hierarchical barriers, making it easier for employees to collaborate and share ideas freely. This sense of camaraderie and mutual respect can lead to more effective teamwork and a more cohesive organizational culture.

Leading companies have recognized the power of play and have integrated it into their corporate cultures. Google, for instance, is renowned for its playful work environment, featuring amenities such as game rooms, nap pods, and communal areas designed to foster interaction and relaxation. This playful atmosphere not only attracts top talent but also cultivates a culture of innovation, where employees feel free to experiment and take risks.

Similarly, LEGO, a company built on the concept of play, incorporates playfulness into its corporate philosophy. LEGO employees are encouraged to engage in playful activities, both individually and in teams, to spark creativity and develop new ideas. This approach has led to continuous innovation and sustained success in a highly competitive market.

Fostering a playful work environment involves creating spaces and opportunities for employees to engage in playful activities. This can include setting aside dedicated areas for relaxation and games, organizing regular team-building events, and incorporating elements of play into daily routines. For example, brainstorming sessions can be transformed into playful workshops where employees use creative tools and techniques to generate ideas.

Leadership plays a crucial role in promoting a culture of play. Leaders who model playful behavior and encourage their teams to take breaks and engage in fun activities set the tone for the rest of the organization. They demonstrate that play is valued and that it is an essential part of the work process, not just a distraction.

The role of play in the workplace is crucial for fostering creativity, innovation, and employee well-being. By integrating play into professional settings, organizations can create a more dynamic, engaging, and productive work environment. As we delve deeper into this chapter, we will explore various techniques for encouraging creativity and innovation, provide examples of creative organizational practices, and offer practical strategies for promoting play at work. Understanding and embracing the role of play can lead to a more vibrant and successful organization, capable of adapting and thriving in an ever-changing business landscape.

Integrating play into professional settings can transform workplace dynamics, fostering a culture of innovation, collaboration, and well-being. While the concept might initially seem counterintuitive to traditional notions of productivity, substantial evidence supports the numerous benefits that play can bring to an organization. Here, we delve deeper into these advantages and explore how they contribute to a thriving business environment.

Enhancing Creativity and Innovation

One of the most significant benefits of integrating play into the workplace is its ability to enhance creativity and innovation. Playful activities stimulate different areas of the brain, encouraging employees to think outside the box and approach problems from new angles. This creative stimulation is essential for generating novel ideas and solutions. Companies like IDEO, a global design and consulting firm, have built their success on fostering a playful culture that encourages experimentation and curiosity. By providing employees with opportunities to engage in playful brainstorming sessions and design thinking workshops, organizations can spur innovation and maintain a competitive edge in their industries.

Reducing Stress and Improving Mental Health

Workplace stress is a pervasive issue that can lead to burnout, decreased productivity, and high employee turnover. Integrating play into the workday offers a powerful antidote to stress. Playful activities provide a mental break from work-related pressures, allowing employees to relax and recharge. This can lead to improved mental health, reduced anxiety, and a more positive outlook on work. For instance, Google's campuses are designed with playful elements such as game rooms, nap pods, and recreational areas, offering employees various ways to unwind and de-stress. These amenities contribute to a healthier, more balanced work environment, enhancing overall well-being.

Fostering Team Cohesion and Collaboration

Play has a unique ability to bring people together and foster a sense of camaraderie. Team-building activities that incorporate play can break down hierarchical barriers and encourage open communication. When employees engage in playful interactions, they build trust and rapport, making it easier to collaborate effectively on work projects. Activities such as group games, team challenges, and social events can strengthen relationships and improve teamwork. At companies like Pixar, playful environments and activities are integral to their creative process, helping to build strong, collaborative teams that produce highly innovative and successful films.

Boosting Employee Engagement and Satisfaction

Employee engagement and job satisfaction are critical factors in organizational success. Playful workplaces can significantly boost engagement by making work more enjoyable and fulfilling. When employees have opportunities to engage in playful activities, they are more likely to feel valued and motivated. This increased engagement leads to higher productivity, better performance, and lower turnover rates. Zappos, known for its fun and quirky company culture, incorporates play into daily operations through spontaneous parades, themed dress-up days, and interactive games. This playful atmosphere contributes to high levels of employee satisfaction and a strong sense of loyalty to the company.

Encouraging Risk-Taking and Resilience

Play encourages a mindset of exploration and experimentation, which is essential for innovation. In a playful environment, employees feel safer to take risks and try new approaches without the fear of failure. This willingness to experiment can lead to significant breakthroughs and creative solutions. Additionally, play fosters resilience by helping employees develop coping strategies and adapt to change. In industries where rapid adaptation is crucial, such as technology and design, a playful culture can provide the flexibility and resilience needed to navigate challenges successfully.

Improving Problem-Solving Skills

Engaging in play can enhance cognitive functions related to problem-solving and critical thinking. Playful activities often require participants to think strategically, make quick decisions, and adapt to new rules or scenarios. These skills are directly transferable to the workplace, where employees must solve complex problems and make informed decisions. For example, hackathons and innovation contests are playful ways to address business challenges, encouraging employees to apply their problem-solving skills creatively and collaboratively.

Attracting and Retaining Talent

A playful and innovative workplace culture can be a significant draw for top talent. In competitive job markets, companies that offer a dynamic and enjoyable work environment stand out to potential employees. Playful workplaces are often perceived as more progressive and employee-centric, making them attractive to individuals seeking meaningful and engaging work experiences. Companies like LinkedIn and Facebook, which are known for their vibrant and playful cultures, have successfully attracted and retained some of the best talents in the tech industry.

Promoting Physical Health

Incorporating physical play into the workplace, such as sports, fitness challenges, or movement-based activities, can promote physical health and wellness. Regular physical activity has numerous benefits, including increased energy levels, improved mood, and better overall health. Encouraging employees to participate in physical play can lead to a more energetic and health-conscious workforce. For instance, Patagonia encourages outdoor activities and sports, aligning with its brand values and promoting a healthy, active lifestyle among its employees.

The benefits of integrating play into professional settings are multifaceted and far-reaching. From enhancing creativity and reducing stress to fostering teamwork and attracting talent, play can transform the workplace into a more dynamic, productive, and enjoyable environment. By embracing the power of play, organizations can cultivate a culture that not only drives business success but also promotes the well-being and satisfaction of their employees. As we explore further in this chapter, understanding how to effectively integrate play and creativity into the workplace can provide valuable insights and practical strategies for fostering a thriving organizational culture.

Fostering creativity and innovation in the workplace involves creating an environment that encourages employees to think outside the box, take risks, and collaborate freely. Organizations can implement several techniques to nurture a culture of creativity and innovation.

Providing employees with the autonomy to explore their ideas is a critical first step. Allowing individuals the freedom to pursue projects that interest them, without micromanagement, can lead to unexpected breakthroughs. Google's "20% time" policy, where employees spend 20% of their workweek on projects of their choosing, has resulted in the development of significant products like Gmail and Google News. Autonomy empowers employees to experiment, innovate, and take ownership of their work.

Creating diverse and stimulating work environments also plays a vital role in fostering creativity. Workspaces designed to inspire, with flexible seating arrangements, open-plan layouts, and dedicated areas for brainstorming, can stimulate creative thinking. These environments should facilitate spontaneous interactions and collaborations among employees from different departments, encouraging the cross-pollination of ideas.

Encouraging cross-functional collaboration is another effective technique. By forming teams with diverse skill sets and perspectives, organizations can tackle problems from various angles, leading to more innovative solutions. At IDEO, project teams are deliberately composed of individuals from different backgrounds, including engineers, designers, and business strategists, to foster a holistic approach to problem-solving.

Implementing programs that celebrate and reward creativity reinforces the importance of innovation within the organization. Recognizing and rewarding employees for their creative contributions, whether through formal awards, promotions, or public acknowledgment, motivates others to think creatively and take risks. This recognition signals that the organization values and supports innovative efforts.

Leadership plays a crucial role in fostering a creative culture. Leaders should model creative behavior by being open to new ideas, encouraging experimentation, and demonstrating a willingness to take calculated risks. They should also provide the necessary resources and support for creative initiatives, including time, funding, and access to tools and technology.

Offering regular training and development opportunities focused on creativity can help employees develop their creative skills. Workshops on design thinking, problem-solving, and creative techniques can equip employees with the tools they need to approach challenges innovatively. These programs should encourage employees to question assumptions, explore new perspectives, and think critically.

Creating a safe space for failure is essential in fostering creativity. Innovation often involves trial and error, and employees must feel safe to fail without fear of negative consequences. Encouraging a mindset that views failures as learning opportunities rather than setbacks can drive more bold and innovative attempts.

Encouraging playful activities and incorporating elements of play into the workday can also stimulate creativity. Playful activities, such as improvisation exercises, brainstorming games, and team-building activities, can break down mental barriers and spark creative thinking. These activities help employees relax, open up, and engage more fully with their creative potential.

Integrating feedback mechanisms into the creative process ensures continuous improvement and refinement of ideas. Constructive feedback helps employees iterate on their ideas, making them more robust and innovative. Regular feedback sessions, peer reviews, and open forums for idea sharing can create a dynamic environment where creativity thrives.

Fostering creativity and innovation requires a multifaceted approach that includes providing autonomy, creating inspiring work environments, encouraging cross-functional collaboration, celebrating creative achievements, and offering leadership support. By implementing these techniques, organizations can cultivate a culture of creativity that drives innovation and positions them for long-term success. Understanding and integrating these strategies into daily operations can transform the workplace into a hub of innovation and creativity, leading to breakthroughs and sustained competitive advantage.

To illustrate how different organizations foster creativity and innovation, we can explore various practices from companies known for their inventive approaches. These examples highlight diverse strategies that have successfully stimulated creative thinking and innovative solutions.

Pixar Animation Studios is renowned for its unique approach to fostering creativity. One of their key practices is the "Braintrust" meetings. During these sessions, filmmakers present their projects to a group of peers who provide candid feedback and constructive criticism. The Braintrust operates on the principles of trust and openness, allowing filmmakers to refine their ideas based on diverse perspectives. This practice has been instrumental in producing consistently high-quality and innovative films.

3M, the multinational conglomerate, encourages creativity through its "15% rule," which allows employees to dedicate 15% of their work time to pursuing their own projects. This policy has led to the development of numerous successful products, including Post-it Notes. By giving employees the freedom to experiment and innovate, 3M has fostered a culture where creativity is a driving force behind its product development.

Atlassian, an enterprise software company, hosts "ShipIt Days" (formerly known as FedEx Days), where employees are given 24 hours to work on any project they choose, often in teams. At the end of the period, teams present their projects to the entire company. These events encourage creativity, teamwork, and rapid prototyping, often resulting in new product features, process improvements, and innovative ideas that benefit the company.

Airbnb fosters creativity through its "Airbnb Design Studio," an internal group that operates like a startup within the company. This studio focuses on exploring new design concepts and user experiences. By providing a dedicated space and resources for creative exploration, Airbnb encourages innovation in both its product offerings and user interfaces. The Design Studio's work has been pivotal in maintaining Airbnb's reputation for cutting-edge design and customer experience.

Adobe has implemented the "Adobe Kickbox" initiative, which provides employees with a physical box containing resources, tools, and guidelines to help them develop and test new ideas. The box includes a prepaid credit card to fund initial experiments and a step-by-step process for turning ideas into viable projects. This initiative empowers employees to take ownership of their creative ideas and provides a structured pathway to innovation.

Spotify employs a "Squad" model for product development, where small, autonomous teams focus on specific features or aspects of the service. Each squad operates like a mini-startup, with the freedom to innovate and make decisions independently. This structure promotes agility and allows teams to quickly iterate and improve their offerings, fostering a dynamic and creative work environment.

LEGO established the "Future Lab," an internal innovation hub tasked with envisioning the future of play. This lab operates separately from the main business units, allowing for greater creative freedom and experimentation. Future Lab's mission is to explore new ideas and technologies that could shape the future of LEGO products. This dedicated focus on innovation has led to groundbreaking products like LEGO Mindstorms and LEGO Ideas.

Salesforce hosts an annual "Dreamforce" event, which includes an "Innovation Summit" where employees and partners can showcase their innovative projects and ideas. This event not only highlights creative achievements but also provides a platform for networking and collaboration. The Innovation Summit encourages a culture of sharing and continuous improvement, driving creativity across the organization.

Valve Corporation, a video game developer and digital distribution company, operates with a flat organizational structure that eliminates traditional hierarchies. Employees are free to choose which projects they want to work on, fostering a high degree of autonomy and creative freedom. This approach has led to the development of highly successful games and innovations in the digital distribution of games.

Facebook (now Meta) holds regular "Hackathons," where employees are encouraged to step away from their daily tasks and work on passion projects. These hackathons have led to the development of several core features and products, including the "Like" button and Facebook Live. By providing a dedicated time and space for creative exploration, Facebook harnesses the innovative potential of its workforce.

These examples demonstrate that fostering creativity within organizations requires intentional practices and a supportive culture. By implementing strategies such as dedicated innovation time, cross-functional collaboration, supportive resources, and open feedback mechanisms, companies can cultivate an environment where creativity and innovation thrive. These practices not only lead to the development of groundbreaking products and solutions but also enhance employee engagement and satisfaction, driving long-term success.

Promoting play and creativity in the workplace involves integrating specific activities and exercises that encourage employees to think outside the box, collaborate, and relax. One effective strategy is to incorporate regular brainstorming sessions where employees are encouraged to share wild and unconventional ideas without the fear of judgment. This can help unlock creative potential and lead to innovative solutions.

Creating dedicated spaces for creativity, such as innovation labs or creative corners, can also make a significant difference. These spaces should be equipped with materials that inspire, such as whiteboards, colorful markers, sticky notes, and prototyping tools. Encouraging employees to take short, frequent breaks in these areas can help refresh their minds and spark new ideas.

Hosting hackathons or innovation challenges can be particularly effective. These events allow employees to step away from their usual tasks and work intensively on creative projects. The collaborative and competitive environment of a hackathon can lead to rapid idea generation and problem-solving. For example, setting aside a day each quarter for a company-wide hackathon can foster a culture of innovation and camaraderie.

Implementing playful activities like improvisational theater exercises can help break down barriers and encourage spontaneous thinking. Improv exercises can improve communication, build team trust, and stimulate creative thinking. These activities push employees to think quickly and adapt, which can translate into more innovative approaches to their work.

Encouraging cross-departmental collaboration can also promote creativity. Setting up regular meetings or collaborative projects between different departments can bring diverse perspectives together, leading to more holistic and innovative solutions. For instance, pairing marketing teams with product development teams can generate new ideas for product features and marketing strategies.

Offering workshops and training sessions focused on creative skills can equip employees with new tools and techniques. Workshops on design thinking, creative problem-solving, and storytelling can provide practical skills that employees can apply to their work. These sessions should be interactive and hands-on, allowing employees to practice and internalize new methods.

Another practical strategy is to organize regular "play breaks" during the workday. These breaks can include activities such as games, puzzles, or physical activities like yoga or dance. Play breaks help employees de-stress, re-energize, and return to their tasks with a fresh perspective. Encouraging a playful atmosphere can also involve informal gatherings, such as themed dress-up days or office decorating contests, which can build team spirit and creativity.

Incorporating feedback loops into the creative process is essential. Regularly soliciting and incorporating feedback from employees can refine and enhance creative initiatives. This could involve holding post-project reviews where teams discuss what worked, what didn't, and how they can improve. Creating a culture where feedback is valued and acted upon ensures that creative processes are continuously evolving.

Allowing for flexible work arrangements can also foster creativity. Giving employees the option to work from different locations or adjust their schedules can lead to a more inspired and productive workforce. Flexibility can reduce stress and provide the mental space needed for creative thinking. Recognizing and celebrating creative efforts is crucial. Highlighting and rewarding innovative ideas, whether through formal awards, public recognition, or tangible rewards, reinforces the importance of creativity in the organization. Celebrations can be part of regular meetings or special events, ensuring that creative achievements are acknowledged and valued.

Promoting play and creativity at work requires a multifaceted approach that includes brainstorming sessions, dedicated creative spaces, hackathons, improv exercises, cross-departmental collaboration, creative workshops, play breaks, feedback loops, flexible work arrangements, and recognition of creative efforts. By integrating these activities and exercises into daily operations, organizations can cultivate an environment where creativity and innovation thrive, leading to sustained success and employee satisfaction.

To ensure that playful and creative initiatives are effective and provide tangible benefits, it is essential to measure their impact. Evaluating these initiatives can help organizations understand their value, refine their approaches, and justify continued investment. Various metrics and methods can be employed to assess the success of these initiatives.
One approach is to use employee engagement surveys. Regularly conducting surveys that include questions about job satisfaction, creativity, and engagement can provide insights into how playful and creative initiatives are affecting the workforce. Higher scores in these areas often correlate with a more motivated and productive workforce. These surveys can be supplemented with

qualitative feedback, where employees provide detailed comments about their experiences and the initiatives' impact on their work.

Another metric is innovation output. This can be measured by tracking the number of new ideas generated, projects initiated, and successful innovations implemented. For example, organizations can monitor the outcomes of hackathons, brainstorming sessions, and innovation labs. Metrics such as the number of patent filings, new product launches, or process improvements can provide concrete evidence of the initiatives' effectiveness.

Productivity and performance metrics are also valuable indicators. Comparing productivity levels and performance metrics before and after the implementation of playful and creative initiatives can reveal their impact. For instance, organizations might see improvements in project completion times, quality of work, or overall efficiency. These metrics can help quantify the benefits of a more engaged and creative workforce.

Employee retention and recruitment rates can serve as indirect measures of the success of these initiatives. High levels of job satisfaction and engagement often lead to lower turnover rates and a stronger ability to attract top talent. Tracking changes in retention rates and analyzing recruitment data can provide insights into how playful and creative initiatives influence organizational appeal and employee loyalty.

Customer satisfaction and feedback can also reflect the impact of these initiatives. Innovation and creativity often lead to better products and services, which in turn enhance customer satisfaction. Surveys and feedback from customers can provide valuable information about how well the organization is meeting their needs and expectations. Improvements in customer satisfaction scores and positive feedback can indicate the success of creative initiatives.

Implementing case studies and success stories within the organization can highlight the qualitative impact of these initiatives. Documenting specific examples where playful and creative approaches have led to significant breakthroughs or improvements can provide compelling evidence of their value. These stories can be shared internally to inspire and motivate employees, as well as externally to showcase the organization's innovative culture.

Monitoring employee health and well-being is another important aspect. Playful and creative initiatives often contribute to reduced stress levels and improved mental health. Tracking metrics such as absenteeism, health-related complaints, and participation in wellness programs can provide insights into the well-being of employees. Improvements in these areas can be linked to the positive effects of a more playful and supportive work environment.

Conducting regular reviews and adjustments to the initiatives is crucial. Establishing a process for ongoing evaluation and refinement ensures that the initiatives remain relevant and effective. This might involve setting up a committee or task force responsible for reviewing feedback, analyzing metrics, and making recommendations for improvements. Regular reviews help maintain momentum and ensure that the initiatives continue to align with organizational goals and employee needs.

Measuring the impact of playful and creative initiatives involves a combination of quantitative and qualitative methods, including employee engagement surveys, innovation output tracking, productivity metrics, retention rates, customer satisfaction, case studies, employee health monitoring, and regular reviews. By systematically evaluating these initiatives, organizations can demonstrate their value, refine their approaches, and create a work environment that fosters sustained creativity, innovation, and overall success. This comprehensive approach to measurement ensures that the benefits of play and creativity are fully realized, contributing to a vibrant and dynamic organizational culture.

Chapter 6: Hybrid Approaches in Organizational Theory

In the evolving landscape of organizational theory, hybrid approaches that combine elements of modern and postmodern paradigms have emerged as powerful strategies. These approaches acknowledge the value of traditional structures while embracing the fluidity and adaptability necessary for contemporary success. This chapter explores the rationale behind hybrid approaches, examines case studies of hybrid organizational models, and provides practical strategies for implementation.

The rationale behind hybrid approaches stems from the need to balance stability with flexibility. Modern organizational structures, with their clear hierarchies and well-defined processes, offer stability, predictability, and control. These elements are crucial for maintaining order and efficiency, particularly in large and complex organizations. However, the rigidity of modern structures can stifle creativity and limit the ability to respond quickly to changing environments.

Postmodern elements, on the other hand, emphasize decentralization, diversity, and adaptability. They foster an environment where innovation can flourish, and organizations can quickly pivot in response to new challenges and opportunities. By integrating these elements, hybrid approaches strive to create organizations that are both stable and agile, capable of sustaining long-term success while adapting to the dynamic nature of the modern business landscape.

Case studies of hybrid organizational models provide valuable insights into how these approaches work in practice. For instance, Haier, a leading appliance manufacturer, has successfully implemented the Rendanheyi model, which combines traditional hierarchical structures with decentralized, autonomous micro-enterprises. This model allows Haier to maintain the benefits of scale and efficiency while fostering innovation and responsiveness at the local level.

Another example is Gore-Tex, known for its lattice organizational structure. This structure integrates the stability of traditional management with the flexibility of a networked approach, allowing for fluid leadership and collaboration across the organization. By leveraging both modern and postmodern principles, Gore-Tex has maintained its position as a leader in innovation within its industry.

Implementing hybrid approaches requires a strategic integration of modern and postmodern principles. Organizations must carefully assess their existing structures and identify areas where flexibility and adaptability can be introduced without compromising core stability. This involves rethinking hierarchical roles, promoting cross-functional teams, and encouraging a culture of continuous learning and innovation.

Tools and frameworks for hybrid organizational development play a crucial role in this process. Frameworks such as the McKinsey 7S model can help organizations align their structure, strategy, systems, shared values, skills, style, and staff to support hybrid approaches. Tools like agile methodologies and design thinking workshops can foster a mindset of experimentation and rapid iteration, essential for blending modern and postmodern elements.

Balancing innovation and tradition is a central challenge in hybrid approaches. Organizations must manage the tension between old and new paradigms, ensuring that innovation does not disrupt core operations and that traditional practices do not stifle new ideas. This balance requires a clear vision and strong leadership to navigate the complexities of integrating diverse elements.

Examples of organizations successfully balancing these elements include IBM, which has integrated agile practices into its traditional corporate structure. This hybrid approach has allowed IBM to innovate rapidly while maintaining its legacy of excellence and reliability. Similarly, Zappos has adopted elements of holacracy within its existing framework, fostering a culture of autonomy and empowerment without abandoning essential managerial oversight.

Hybrid approaches in organizational theory offer a compelling way to combine the strengths of modern and postmodern paradigms. By integrating stability with flexibility, these approaches enable organizations to navigate the complexities of the contemporary business environment effectively. As we delve deeper into this chapter, we will explore detailed strategies for implementing hybrid models, examine tools and frameworks for development, and highlight more examples of organizations that have successfully embraced this innovative approach. Understanding and applying these principles can help organizations achieve a dynamic balance, fostering sustainable growth and resilience in a rapidly changing world.

The rationale behind hybrid approaches in organizational theory lies in the necessity to balance stability and flexibility in today's complex business environment. Traditional modern structures offer clear hierarchies, well-defined roles, and established processes that provide order, predictability, and control. These characteristics are essential for maintaining efficiency, ensuring consistent quality, and managing large-scale operations. However, the rigidity inherent in these structures can impede creativity, slow response times to market changes, and limit the organization's ability to innovate.

In contrast, postmodern elements prioritize decentralization, diversity, and adaptability. These elements foster environments where innovation thrives, and organizations can swiftly pivot in response to emerging challenges and opportunities. Postmodern approaches often emphasize flatter structures, cross-functional teams, and an open culture that values diverse perspectives and continuous learning. While these characteristics can enhance agility and creativity, they may also lead to a lack of coherence and consistency, which can be detrimental to large or highly regulated organizations.

Hybrid methods seek to combine the best of both worlds, integrating the stability of modern structures with the adaptability of postmodern elements. This integration allows organizations to maintain the efficiencies and control necessary for operational excellence while embedding the flexibility required for innovation and rapid response to change.

One key rationale for hybrid approaches is the dynamic nature of today's business environment. Rapid technological advancements, globalization, and shifting consumer preferences demand that organizations be both resilient and responsive. Modern structures alone may not provide the necessary agility, while purely postmodern approaches may lack the stability to scale and sustain long-term growth. By blending these paradigms, organizations can achieve a balance that supports both immediate adaptability and long-term sustainability.

Another important rationale is the need for inclusivity and employee engagement. Modern hierarchical structures can often lead to siloed departments and top-down decision-making, which may disengage employees and stifle their creativity. Postmodern elements, with their emphasis on decentralized decision-making and cross-functional collaboration, can enhance employee empowerment and engagement. When employees feel their contributions are valued and their ideas can lead to tangible changes, they are more likely to be motivated and committed to the organization's success. Moreover, hybrid approaches can better cater to diverse organizational needs. Different departments or functions within an organization might require different management styles. For instance, research and development teams might benefit from the flexibility and creativity encouraged by postmodern elements, while production and operations might rely on the predictability and control provided by modern structures. A hybrid approach allows for tailored management practices that align with the specific needs and dynamics of various teams and functions within the organization.

The evolution of hybrid approaches also reflects broader societal changes. As workforces become more diverse and the lines between work and personal life blur, there is a growing demand for workplaces that are both structured and flexible. Employees today seek environments where they can thrive both professionally and personally, and hybrid models can provide the necessary framework to support this balance.

The rationale behind hybrid approaches in organizational theory is to create resilient, innovative, and adaptive organizations capable of navigating the complexities of the modern business landscape. By combining the stability of modern elements with the flexibility of postmodern principles, organizations can build structures that are robust enough to handle scale and complexity, yet agile enough to adapt to change and foster continuous innovation. This balanced approach not only supports organizational success but also enhances employee engagement, satisfaction, and overall well-being.

Exploring case studies of organizations that have successfully implemented hybrid models can provide valuable insights into how these approaches function in practice. These examples illustrate how companies can blend modern and postmodern elements to create structures that balance stability and flexibility, driving both efficiency and innovation.

IBM

IBM has long been recognized for its ability to adapt and evolve. Traditionally known for its hierarchical structure and process-oriented approach, IBM has integrated agile methodologies into its operations to enhance flexibility and innovation. By adopting agile practices, such as Scrum and Kanban, within its product development teams, IBM has fostered a more collaborative and responsive environment. This hybrid model allows IBM to maintain the operational efficiency required for its large-scale operations while promoting the agility needed to innovate and respond to market changes rapidly.

Unilever

Unilever, a global consumer goods company, has adopted a hybrid organizational model that combines centralized control with decentralized operations. While strategic decisions and brand management are centralized to ensure consistency and leverage economies of scale, Unilever empowers regional teams to make decisions tailored to local markets. This approach allows the company to maintain a coherent global strategy while being agile and responsive to local consumer needs. The balance between global oversight and local autonomy has enabled Unilever to achieve significant growth and remain competitive across diverse markets.

GE (General Electric)

General Electric has historically been a model of modern organizational principles, with a strong emphasis on hierarchy and process efficiency. However, under the leadership of former CEO Jeff Immelt, GE began to incorporate elements of the Lean Startup methodology. GE launched the FastWorks program, which applied Lean Startup principles to product development, encouraging teams to work in small, cross-functional units that could iterate quickly and respond to customer feedback. This hybrid approach allowed GE to maintain its traditional strengths in operational efficiency while fostering a more innovative and agile culture.

Spotify

Spotify, a leading music streaming service, uses a hybrid model known as the "Spotify Model," which integrates agile methodologies with a flexible, decentralized structure. The company is organized into autonomous squads, each responsible for a specific aspect of the product. These squads operate within larger tribes, which are aligned by product area. Chapters and guilds, which cut across squads and tribes, ensure consistency in practices and knowledge sharing. This hybrid approach combines the agility and autonomy of a postmodern structure with the coherence and alignment provided by modern organizational elements.

Haier

Haier, a Chinese multinational consumer electronics and home appliances company, has implemented the Rendanheyi model, which combines hierarchical structures with decentralized micro-enterprises. Each micro-enterprise operates as an independent entity with its own profit and loss responsibilities, allowing for greater innovation and responsiveness. At the same time, Haier maintains centralized control over strategic decisions and brand management, ensuring alignment with the company's overall vision and goals. This hybrid model has enabled Haier to achieve rapid growth and maintain its competitive edge in a highly dynamic market.

Cisco Systems

Cisco Systems, a leader in networking and telecommunications, has adopted a hybrid approach to manage its complex global operations. While Cisco maintains a traditional hierarchical structure for core functions like finance and operations, it uses cross-functional teams and collaborative platforms for innovation and product development. This approach allows Cisco to leverage its scale and operational efficiency while promoting a culture of collaboration and agility. The use of technology and digital tools facilitates seamless communication and coordination across different parts of the organization.

Procter & Gamble (P&G)

Procter & Gamble, one of the largest consumer goods companies in the world, has integrated modern and postmodern elements to create a hybrid organizational model. P&G maintains centralized control over key functions such as brand management and global strategy while empowering individual business units to operate with a high degree of autonomy. This structure allows P&G to ensure consistency and leverage synergies across its portfolio while fostering innovation and responsiveness at the local level. The company's use of digital tools and data analytics further enhances its ability to balance these elements effectively.

Zappos

Zappos, an online shoe and clothing retailer, has implemented elements of holacracy within its existing framework. Holacracy is a decentralized management system that distributes decision-making authority across self-organizing teams. At Zappos, this approach has created a more flexible and adaptive organizational structure, fostering a culture of autonomy and empowerment. While the company retains some traditional hierarchical elements for critical functions, the integration of holacracy principles has allowed Zappos to maintain its innovative edge and unique company culture.

These case studies demonstrate the diverse ways in which organizations can implement hybrid models to balance stability and flexibility. By integrating modern and postmodern elements, these companies have created structures that support both operational efficiency and continuous innovation. Understanding these examples can provide valuable insights for other organizations looking to adopt hybrid approaches and achieve similar success.

Integrating modern and postmodern principles into an organizational structure requires a strategic approach that balances stability with flexibility. This process involves several key steps to ensure that both elements complement each other effectively, fostering an environment where innovation and efficiency can thrive simultaneously.

Begin by evaluating the current state of the organization, identifying areas where traditional structures support stability and where flexibility is needed to foster innovation. Conduct surveys, interviews, and focus groups with employees at all levels to understand their needs and the organizational culture. This assessment will help in tailoring the hybrid approach to fit the specific context of the organization.

Establish clear objectives and a vision for integrating modern and postmodern principles. This vision should articulate the benefits of a hybrid approach, such as increased agility, enhanced innovation, and sustained operational efficiency. Communicate this vision to all stakeholders to build buy-in and ensure alignment with the organization's strategic goals.

Design an organizational structure that incorporates both hierarchical and decentralized elements. For instance, maintain traditional hierarchies for core functions like finance, HR, and compliance, which benefit from clear processes and controls. Simultaneously, create cross-functional teams or units with more autonomy and flexibility to drive innovation and respond to market changes. These teams should be empowered to make decisions quickly and operate with a degree of independence.

Adopt agile methodologies to enhance flexibility and responsiveness within the organization. Agile practices, such as Scrum and Kanban, encourage iterative development, continuous feedback, and adaptive planning. Integrate these practices into project management and product development processes to foster a culture of experimentation and rapid iteration. Training and workshops on agile principles can help teams understand and embrace these methodologies.

Promote a culture that values collaboration, continuous learning, and open communication. Encourage employees to share ideas and collaborate across functions and levels. Implement tools and platforms that facilitate communication and knowledge sharing, such as collaborative software and internal social networks. Regular training programs and workshops focused on creative problem-solving and innovation can further reinforce this culture.

Leverage digital tools and technologies to support the integration of modern and postmodern principles. Tools like project management software, collaborative platforms, and data analytics can enhance both operational efficiency and innovation. These technologies enable real-time communication, streamline workflows, and provide insights that inform decision-making. Ensure that employees are trained to use these tools effectively.

Equip leaders and middle managers with the skills and knowledge to balance modern and postmodern elements. Provide training on adaptive leadership, change management, and fostering innovation. Leaders should model the desired behaviors, demonstrating a commitment to both stability and flexibility. Empowered leaders can drive the cultural and structural changes needed to implement a hybrid approach successfully.

Start by piloting the hybrid approach in select departments or teams. Monitor the outcomes, gather feedback, and make necessary adjustments before scaling the model organization-wide. This gradual implementation allows for testing and refining the approach, ensuring that it meets the organization's needs and objectives.

Define metrics to evaluate the success of the hybrid approach. These might include measures of innovation output, employee engagement, productivity, and customer satisfaction. Regularly monitor these metrics and review progress to ensure that the integration of modern and postmodern principles is achieving the desired outcomes. Use this data to make informed adjustments and improvements.

Create mechanisms for ongoing feedback and continuous improvement. Encourage employees to provide feedback on the hybrid approach and suggest improvements. Regularly review and refine processes, structures, and practices to ensure they remain aligned with organizational goals and evolving needs. This iterative process helps sustain the benefits of a hybrid approach over the long term.

Integrating modern and postmodern principles into an organizational structure requires a thoughtful and strategic approach. By assessing organizational needs, defining clear objectives, creating a balanced structure, implementing agile methodologies, fostering a collaborative culture, leveraging digital tools, empowering leadership, piloting and scaling gradually, establishing metrics, and encouraging continuous improvement, organizations can successfully blend stability and flexibility. This hybrid approach not only enhances operational efficiency but also drives innovation and adaptability, positioning the organization for sustained success in a dynamic business environment.

Integrating modern and postmodern principles in organizational development necessitates the use of various tools and frameworks that facilitate both stability and flexibility. One effective framework is the McKinsey 7S model, which helps organizations align their structure, strategy, systems, shared values, skills, style, and staff to support hybrid approaches. This comprehensive model ensures that all elements of the organization are harmonized and can effectively incorporate both traditional and innovative practices.

Agile methodologies, such as Scrum and Kanban, offer practical tools for enhancing flexibility and responsiveness. These methodologies encourage iterative development, continuous feedback, and adaptive planning, fostering a culture of experimentation and rapid iteration. By integrating agile practices into project management and product development processes, organizations can create a more dynamic and responsive environment.

Design thinking is another valuable framework for hybrid organizational development. This human-centered approach to innovation focuses on understanding user needs, generating creative solutions, and iteratively testing and refining ideas. Design thinking workshops and training sessions can equip employees with the skills to approach problems creatively and collaboratively, driving innovation throughout the organization.

Collaborative platforms and digital tools are essential for supporting hybrid structures. Tools like Microsoft Teams, Slack, and Trello facilitate real-time communication and collaboration, enabling teams to work together seamlessly across different locations and functions. These platforms support both the hierarchical and decentralized elements of a hybrid approach, ensuring that information flows efficiently and decisions can be made quickly.

Balanced scorecards provide a framework for tracking and measuring the performance of hybrid initiatives. This tool helps organizations translate their vision and strategy into specific, measurable objectives across multiple perspectives, including financial, customer, internal processes, and learning and growth. By regularly monitoring these metrics, organizations can assess the effectiveness of their hybrid approach and make data-driven adjustments.

Lean management principles, which focus on maximizing value and minimizing waste, can also be integrated into hybrid organizational development. Lean tools such as value stream mapping and continuous improvement cycles help streamline processes and enhance operational efficiency while maintaining the flexibility needed for innovation. By adopting lean practices, organizations can balance stability and adaptability, creating a more efficient and responsive operation.

Holacracy is a management framework that distributes decision-making authority across self-organizing teams. While it may not be suitable for every organization, elements of holacracy can be adapted to create a more flexible and empowered workforce. By defining clear roles and responsibilities and encouraging autonomy, organizations can foster a culture of accountability and innovation.

Balanced governance structures are crucial for managing the tension between traditional and innovative elements. Creating committees or councils that include representatives from various levels and functions can ensure that both stability and flexibility are maintained. These governance bodies can oversee the integration of modern and postmodern principles, address challenges, and ensure alignment with the organization's overall strategy.

Regular feedback mechanisms are vital for continuous improvement. Establishing processes for gathering and acting on feedback from employees, customers, and other stakeholders ensures that the hybrid approach remains effective and relevant. Tools like employee surveys, customer feedback platforms, and performance reviews provide valuable insights that can inform ongoing adjustments and enhancements.

Balancing innovation and tradition involves managing the tension between established practices and new approaches. This balance is crucial for organizations that want to remain competitive and relevant while maintaining the stability that traditional methods provide. Successfully integrating these paradigms requires a strategic approach that acknowledges the value of both.

A key aspect of managing this tension is fostering a culture that values both innovation and tradition. Leadership plays a vital role in modeling this balance by showing appreciation for past successes and encouraging forward-thinking initiatives. This dual focus helps create an environment where employees feel secure in exploring new ideas while respecting established processes.

Another critical element is clear communication. Organizations must articulate the reasons for integrating new approaches and how they complement traditional methods. Transparent communication helps build trust and reduces resistance to change, as employees understand the benefits and rationale behind new initiatives.

Flexible structures are essential for balancing innovation and tradition. Creating cross-functional teams that blend experienced employees with newer, more innovative thinkers can bridge the gap between old and new paradigms. These teams can leverage the expertise and stability provided by traditional methods while incorporating fresh perspectives and creative solutions.

Implementing pilot programs allows organizations to test innovative ideas on a small scale before rolling them out more broadly. This approach mitigates risk and provides valuable insights into how new practices can be integrated with existing ones. Successful pilots can then be scaled up, ensuring a smoother transition and wider acceptance.

Ongoing training and development are crucial for equipping employees with the skills needed to navigate both traditional and innovative practices. Offering training programs that cover new technologies, methodologies, and creative problem-solving techniques ensures that the workforce is well-prepared to embrace change while maintaining core competencies.

Incentivizing innovation while recognizing the importance of tradition is another effective strategy. Reward systems that celebrate both innovative ideas and adherence to proven practices can motivate employees to contribute to both areas. This balanced approach ensures that the organization values stability and creativity equally.

Regular feedback and review processes help maintain the balance between innovation and tradition. Soliciting input from employees at all levels provides insights into what is working and where adjustments are needed. These feedback loops ensure that the organization can continuously refine its approach, blending the best of both worlds.

Leadership must also be adaptable and open to change. Leaders should demonstrate a willingness to pivot when necessary, showing that they value innovation without abandoning the principles that have contributed to the organization's success. This adaptability fosters a culture of continuous improvement and resilience.

Balancing innovation and tradition requires a multifaceted approach that includes fostering a supportive culture, clear communication, flexible structures, pilot programs, ongoing training, incentivization, regular feedback, and adaptable leadership. By strategically managing the tension between old and new paradigms, organizations can create an environment that leverages the strengths of both, driving sustained success and growth. This balance enables companies to remain competitive in a rapidly changing landscape while honoring the stability that traditional methods provide.

Examples of organizations successfully balancing innovation and tradition illustrate how a strategic approach can create a dynamic and resilient environment. One such organization is 3M, renowned for its commitment to innovation while maintaining strong traditional foundations. 3M encourages a culture of experimentation through its "15% rule," allowing employees to dedicate a portion of their time to pursuing creative projects. This initiative has led to the development of numerous breakthrough products, including Post-it Notes, while preserving the company's core principles of quality and reliability.

Toyota exemplifies another successful balance between tradition and innovation. The Toyota Production System (TPS) is rooted in traditional manufacturing principles of efficiency and continuous improvement, known as "kaizen." At the same time, Toyota embraces innovative practices, such as the introduction of hybrid and electric vehicles, and continuous advancements in manufacturing technology. This blend of maintaining rigorous quality standards while pushing the boundaries of automotive innovation has kept Toyota at the forefront of the industry.

Johnson & Johnson, a global leader in healthcare, effectively combines its long-standing commitment to patient care and safety with innovative approaches to research and development. The company leverages its extensive experience and robust ethical standards while investing heavily in cutting-edge technologies and treatments. This dual focus allows Johnson & Johnson to uphold its tradition of trust and reliability while leading advancements in medical science.

Nestlé, the world's largest food and beverage company, demonstrates a successful integration of tradition and innovation by continually evolving its product offerings to meet changing consumer demands while maintaining its commitment to quality and sustainability. Nestlé invests in research and development to create new products that cater to modern health trends and environmental concerns, such as plant-based alternatives and sustainable packaging solutions. This approach ensures that Nestlé stays relevant in a competitive market while honoring its legacy of quality and nutritional excellence.

General Electric (GE) also exemplifies a balanced approach through its blend of traditional industrial expertise and innovative practices. GE's FastWorks program applies lean startup principles to its traditionally structured business units, fostering a more agile and responsive organizational culture. This program encourages teams to experiment, iterate, and learn quickly, helping GE maintain its competitive edge in the rapidly evolving technology landscape while leveraging its industrial heritage.

Procter & Gamble (P&G) integrates tradition and innovation by maintaining its rigorous brand management practices while embracing digital transformation and consumer insights. P&G uses advanced analytics and data-driven decision-making to understand consumer preferences and drive product innovation. This approach allows the company to adapt to changing market conditions and consumer behaviors without compromising its well-established standards of quality and brand consistency.

Lego Group exemplifies a company that successfully balances its rich history with innovative product development. While rooted in its iconic building blocks, Lego continually reinvents itself by incorporating new themes, digital technologies, and interactive experiences. Initiatives like Lego Mindstorms and Lego Ideas engage consumers in the creative process, blending traditional play with modern innovation to keep the brand relevant and exciting.

IBM's transformation over the years showcases the balance between maintaining traditional strengths and embracing new opportunities. Known for its legacy in hardware and mainframe computing, IBM has successfully shifted its focus to cloud computing, artificial intelligence, and blockchain technology.

This strategic pivot allows IBM to leverage its historical expertise while positioning itself as a leader in emerging technologies.

These examples highlight the diverse ways organizations can effectively balance tradition and innovation. By fostering a culture that values both stability and flexibility, leveraging core strengths while embracing new ideas, and maintaining clear communication and adaptable leadership, these companies demonstrate that it is possible to thrive in a rapidly changing business landscape. Successfully integrating modern and postmodern principles enables organizations to navigate complexities, drive sustained growth, and remain competitive while honoring their foundational values and legacy.

Chapter 7: Adapting to the Global Landscape

The global business environment today is characterized by unprecedented complexity, dynamism, and interconnectivity. Rapid technological advancements, shifting geopolitical landscapes, and evolving consumer preferences are reshaping how businesses operate and compete. As organizations navigate this multifaceted terrain, they face numerous challenges and opportunities that require strategic adaptation and innovative thinking.

One of the most significant challenges in the global business environment is managing the impact of technological disruption. Emerging technologies such as artificial intelligence, blockchain, and the Internet of Things are transforming industries and business models. Organizations must continuously innovate and adapt to remain competitive, leveraging these technologies to improve efficiency, enhance customer experiences, and create new revenue streams. However, the rapid pace of technological change also presents risks, including cybersecurity threats, data privacy concerns, and the need for ongoing investment in digital infrastructure and skills development.

Geopolitical volatility is another critical factor shaping the global business landscape. Trade tensions, regulatory changes, and political instability in key markets can disrupt supply chains, impact market access, and create uncertainty for businesses. Organizations must develop robust risk management strategies and cultivate flexibility to navigate these uncertainties. Building strong relationships with local stakeholders, diversifying supply chains, and staying informed about geopolitical developments are essential for mitigating risks and capitalizing on opportunities in different regions.

Sustainability and environmental responsibility are increasingly important considerations for global businesses. Climate change, resource scarcity, and growing environmental awareness among consumers and regulators are driving the need for sustainable business practices. Companies are expected to reduce their carbon footprints, adopt circular economy principles, and ensure responsible sourcing of materials. Embracing sustainability not only mitigates risks but also creates opportunities for innovation and differentiation, as consumers increasingly prefer environmentally responsible brands.

The global workforce is becoming more diverse and distributed, presenting both challenges and opportunities for organizations. Talent shortages in critical areas, such as technology and data science, require businesses to adopt innovative approaches to talent acquisition and development. Remote work and flexible working arrangements, accelerated by the COVID-19 pandemic, have become standard practices in many industries. Organizations must foster inclusive cultures, provide opportunities for continuous learning, and implement technologies that support collaboration and productivity across geographically dispersed teams.

Consumer preferences and behaviors are evolving rapidly, influenced by digitalization, demographic shifts, and cultural trends. Businesses must stay attuned to these changes and adapt their products, services, and marketing strategies accordingly. Personalization, convenience, and seamless omnichannel experiences are becoming essential components of customer expectations. Leveraging data analytics and customer insights allows organizations to tailor their offerings and engage more effectively with their target audiences.

Economic inequality and social justice issues are gaining prominence on the global business agenda. Companies are increasingly held accountable for their social impact and expected to contribute positively to society. This includes addressing issues such as fair labor practices, diversity and inclusion, and community engagement. Organizations that demonstrate a commitment to social responsibility can enhance their reputations, build stronger relationships with stakeholders, and attract and retain talent.

Globalization continues to drive economic integration, creating opportunities for businesses to expand into new markets and access a broader customer base. However, this also brings challenges related to cultural differences, regulatory compliance, and competition from local players. Successful global expansion requires a deep understanding of local markets, the ability to adapt business models and strategies, and the development of strong local partnerships.

The rise of digital platforms and ecosystems is transforming how businesses interact with customers, partners, and competitors. Companies can leverage these platforms to create new business models, enhance customer engagement, and drive innovation. However, this also requires navigating complex ecosystems, managing data privacy and security issues, and staying agile in a rapidly evolving digital landscape.

Cultural awareness is not just an asset but a necessity. Understanding and respecting cultural differences can significantly influence the success of international ventures. Cultural awareness helps businesses navigate the complexities of cross-cultural communication, foster effective collaboration, and build strong relationships with diverse stakeholders.

Businesses frequently operate across multiple countries, each with its own set of cultural norms, values, and business practices. Ignoring these differences can lead to misunderstandings, miscommunications, and conflicts that can jeopardize business relationships and transactions. On the other hand, companies that demonstrate cultural awareness can build trust, enhance cooperation, and create a more inclusive work environment, which can lead to greater innovation and competitive advantage.

For instance, marketing campaigns that resonate well in one culture may fail or even backfire in another if cultural nuances are not considered. Similarly, management practices effective in one country might be perceived as inappropriate or offensive in another. Therefore, being culturally aware enables businesses to tailor their strategies to fit the cultural context, leading to more successful outcomes.

Fostering cultural sensitivity within an organization involves deliberate efforts to educate and empower employees, as well as to integrate cultural awareness into business operations and strategies. Here are several strategies to achieve this:

Cultural Training Programs: Implementing comprehensive cultural training programs is essential for raising awareness and understanding among employees. These programs can cover various aspects of cultural differences, such as communication styles, negotiation tactics, decision-making processes, and social norms. By providing employees with the knowledge and tools to navigate cultural differences, businesses can enhance cross-cultural interactions and reduce the risk of misunderstandings.

Diverse Teams: Building diverse teams that include members from different cultural backgrounds can foster a more inclusive and culturally sensitive environment. Diverse teams bring varied perspectives and ideas, which can lead to more innovative solutions and better decision-making. Encouraging collaboration and open dialogue among team members helps to build mutual respect and understanding.

Local Expertise: Leveraging local expertise is crucial when expanding into new markets. Hiring local employees or consultants who understand the cultural context can provide invaluable insights and guidance. These local experts can help businesses navigate regulatory environments, understand consumer behavior, and adapt their strategies to align with local customs and preferences.

Inclusive Leadership: Leaders play a pivotal role in fostering cultural sensitivity. Inclusive leadership involves recognizing and valuing cultural differences, promoting open communication, and encouraging diverse viewpoints. Leaders should model culturally sensitive behavior and create an environment where employees feel comfortable expressing their cultural identities.

Cross-Cultural Communication: Effective cross-cultural communication is key to fostering cultural sensitivity. Businesses should promote clear and respectful communication practices that consider cultural nuances. This includes being mindful of language barriers, using inclusive language, and being aware of non-verbal cues. Encouraging active listening and empathy can also enhance cross-cultural understanding.

Cultural Exchange Programs: Implementing cultural exchange programs can provide employees with firsthand experience of different cultures. These programs can include short-term assignments, international rotations, or cultural immersion trips. Such experiences help employees develop a deeper appreciation of cultural diversity and enhance their ability to work effectively in global teams.

Adaptation of Business Practices: Adapting business practices to align with local cultural norms is essential for success in international markets. This may involve modifying marketing strategies, product offerings, or management approaches to fit the cultural context. For example, a company entering an Asian market might emphasize group harmony and long-term relationships in its business dealings, reflecting local cultural values.

Continuous Learning and Feedback: Fostering cultural sensitivity is an ongoing process. Businesses should encourage continuous learning and improvement by seeking feedback from employees and stakeholders about cultural interactions. Regularly reviewing and updating cultural training programs, policies, and practices ensures that the organization remains responsive to cultural changes and emerging trends.

Cultural Sensitivity Metrics: Establishing metrics to measure cultural sensitivity can help organizations track progress and identify areas for improvement. These metrics might include employee engagement surveys, diversity and inclusion indices, and feedback from international partners and customers. Using these metrics, businesses can make informed decisions about how to enhance cultural sensitivity across the organization.

Cultural awareness and sensitivity are crucial components of success in the global business environment. By implementing strategies such as cultural training programs, building diverse teams, leveraging local expertise, promoting inclusive leadership, and adapting business practices, organizations can foster a culturally sensitive and adaptable workforce. This not only enhances cross-cultural interactions but also drives innovation, improves decision-making, and strengthens global business relationships. Embracing cultural diversity and fostering sensitivity can ultimately lead to more sustainable and successful international ventures.

Coca-Cola's "Think Global, Act Local" Strategy

Coca-Cola is a prime example of a company that has successfully implemented a global strategy while adapting to local markets. Their "Think Global, Act Local" approach allows the company to maintain a consistent global brand image while tailoring products and marketing strategies to fit local tastes and preferences. In Japan, for instance, Coca-Cola introduced unique products like green tea-flavored Coke and seasonal beverages that align with local tastes. This strategy not only boosts sales but also strengthens the brand's relevance in diverse markets.

McDonald's Global Localization

McDonald's has mastered the art of global localization, offering a menu that resonates with local tastes and cultural preferences while maintaining its core brand identity. In India, where a significant portion of the population is vegetarian and beef consumption is taboo, McDonald's offers a range of vegetarian options and chicken-based products. The McAloo Tikki, a popular vegetarian burger, caters specifically to local tastes. This ability to adapt to local preferences while maintaining a consistent global brand has been crucial to McDonald's success worldwide.

Unilever's Sustainable Living Plan

Unilever's Sustainable Living Plan (USLP) is a global initiative aimed at reducing the company's environmental footprint and increasing its positive social impact. Launched in 2010, the USLP sets ambitious goals, including reducing greenhouse gas emissions, improving water use efficiency, and enhancing the livelihoods of millions of people through sustainable sourcing practices. Unilever's commitment to sustainability has driven innovation and efficiency across its global operations, from sourcing raw materials to reducing waste in production. This initiative not only addresses global challenges but also resonates with consumers who increasingly prioritize sustainability.

Apple's Global Supply Chain Management

Apple's approach to global supply chain management exemplifies how to effectively manage a complex, global network. By building strong relationships with suppliers around the world and investing in state-of-the-art manufacturing processes, Apple ensures high standards of quality and efficiency. The company's rigorous supplier code of conduct includes standards for labor practices, environmental responsibility, and ethics, ensuring that all suppliers adhere to the same high standards. This global initiative has allowed Apple to maintain product consistency and quality while scaling its operations to meet global demand.

Starbucks' Global Ethos

Starbucks has successfully expanded globally by maintaining its core brand values while adapting to local cultures. The company's commitment to ethically sourcing coffee and supporting local communities is central to its global strategy. In China, Starbucks has integrated elements of local tea culture into its product offerings, while in the Middle East, the company has adapted store designs to respect local customs and traditions. Starbucks' global ethos of ethical sourcing, community engagement, and cultural sensitivity has been key to its international success.

Siemens' Global Research and Development Network

Siemens, a global leader in technology and engineering, has established a robust global research and development (R&D) network to drive innovation. With R&D centers strategically located around the world, Siemens leverages local talent and expertise to develop cutting-edge technologies. This global R&D network fosters collaboration across borders, allowing Siemens to stay at the forefront of technological advancements. By integrating global insights and expertise, Siemens ensures that its innovations are relevant and competitive in diverse markets.

Toyota's Lean Manufacturing System

Toyota's lean manufacturing system, known as the Toyota Production System (TPS), has been successfully implemented across its global operations. This system focuses on eliminating waste, optimizing processes, and continuously improving efficiency and quality. TPS has been adapted to various cultural contexts while maintaining its core principles, allowing Toyota to produce high-quality vehicles efficiently and consistently. The global implementation of TPS has been instrumental in Toyota's reputation for reliability and innovation.

Nestlé's Creating Shared Value (CSV) Strategy

Nestlé's Creating Shared Value (CSV) strategy focuses on generating economic and social value simultaneously. This global initiative addresses critical issues such as nutrition, water, and rural development. In Africa, Nestlé has implemented programs to improve agricultural practices, ensuring a sustainable supply chain while enhancing the livelihoods of local farmers. By aligning its business goals with social and environmental objectives, Nestlé creates long-term value for both the company and the communities it operates in.

GE's Ecomagination Initiative

General Electric's Ecomagination initiative is a global effort to develop and promote environmentally sustainable technologies. Launched in 2005, the initiative focuses on reducing environmental impact through innovation in energy efficiency, renewable energy, and water management. Ecomagination has driven GE to invest in clean technology and sustainable practices across its global operations. This initiative not only addresses pressing environmental challenges but also opens new markets and opportunities for GE's products and services.

DHL's Global Connectedness Index

DHL's Global Connectedness Index (GCI) is an initiative that measures and analyzes globalization trends by tracking international flows of trade, capital, information, and people. The GCI provides insights into how countries and regions are interconnected and how these connections impact global business. By leveraging this data, DHL enhances its logistics services, ensuring that they meet the needs of a globally interconnected world. This initiative helps businesses navigate the complexities of globalization and optimize their international operations.

These case studies demonstrate how successful global initiatives can address diverse challenges and capitalize on opportunities. By understanding and adapting to local cultures, prioritizing sustainability, leveraging global networks, and driving innovation, these companies have achieved remarkable success in the global business environment. These examples provide valuable lessons for other organizations seeking to thrive in an increasingly interconnected and dynamic world.

As we look ahead, the future of post-postmodern leadership promises to be dynamic, adaptive, and deeply integrated with the complexities of the global business environment. Post-postmodern leadership, also known as metamodernism or digimodernism, represents a synthesis of modernist and postmodernist principles, fostering a leadership style that embraces both the stability of traditional structures and the fluidity required for innovation and adaptability.

The post-postmodern leader is characterized by a pragmatic approach that balances skepticism with constructive frameworks. These leaders understand the importance of acknowledging the complexity and fluidity of modern organizations while providing practical solutions that drive growth and innovation. In an era where change is constant, post-postmodern leaders are adept at navigating uncertainty and leveraging it as a catalyst for transformation.

One of the hallmarks of post-postmodern leadership is its emphasis on networks and relationships. Modern organizations are increasingly seen as dynamic networks of interconnected actors rather than rigid hierarchies. Leaders must foster strong, collaborative relationships both within and outside the organization, recognizing that these networks are crucial for achieving strategic objectives and driving innovation. Building and maintaining trust, reciprocity, and effective communication within these networks are fundamental to the success of post-postmodern leadership.

Ethical considerations are paramount in post-postmodern leadership. There is a renewed focus on developing non-deontological ethical approaches that go beyond rigid rules and emphasize flexibility, context-sensitivity, and responsiveness. Leaders must navigate ethical dilemmas with a nuanced understanding, ensuring that decisions are not only legally compliant but also morally sound and socially responsible. The increasing importance of corporate social responsibility and sustainable business practices aligns well with the ethical focus of post-postmodern leadership.

Adaptive leadership is another critical component of post-postmodernism. The rapidly changing business landscape demands leaders who are flexible, resilient, and capable of embracing complexity and uncertainty. Post-postmodern leaders must cultivate an organizational culture that encourages experimentation, learning from failure, and continuous improvement. This adaptability enables organizations to pivot quickly in response to market shifts and emerging opportunities.

Distributed leadership marks a departure from traditional top-down models. In a post-postmodern context, leadership is more collaborative and networked, reflecting the interconnected nature of modern organizations. This approach empowers employees at all levels to take on leadership roles, fostering a sense of ownership and engagement. By leveraging the collective intelligence of the organization, distributed leadership drives innovation and enhances decision-making processes.

The integration of technology is a defining feature of post-postmodern leadership. Leaders must understand and leverage digital tools to enhance organizational efficiency, communication, and innovation. The ability to harness the power of data analytics, artificial intelligence, and other technological advancements is essential for maintaining a competitive edge. Moreover, leaders must address the ethical and societal implications of technology, ensuring that digital transformation aligns with broader organizational values and goals.

Cultural sensitivity and adaptation are crucial in a globalized business environment. Post-postmodern leaders must be adept at navigating diverse cultural landscapes, understanding local nuances, and fostering inclusive environments. This cultural awareness not only enhances global operations but also drives employee engagement and satisfaction. By valuing diversity and promoting inclusivity, leaders can create a more innovative and resilient organization.

The future of post-postmodern leadership also involves balancing innovation and tradition. Leaders must manage the tension between established practices and new approaches, ensuring that the organization remains both stable and agile. This balance requires a clear vision, effective communication, and adaptable leadership. By integrating modern and postmodern elements, leaders can create a dynamic organizational culture that supports both efficiency and innovation.

The future of post-postmodern leadership is characterized by its ability to embrace complexity, foster collaboration, and drive ethical and adaptive practices. As organizations navigate the challenges and opportunities of the global business environment, post-postmodern leaders will play a pivotal role in shaping resilient, innovative, and socially responsible enterprises. By combining the strengths of traditional and contemporary leadership paradigms, post-postmodern leaders are well-equipped to guide their organizations toward sustainable success in an ever-evolving landscape.

In the context and relevance of post-postmodernism, we explored how this leadership approach transcends the skepticism of postmodernism to offer constructive frameworks. Emphasizing networks and relationships, ethical considerations, adaptive leadership, and the integration of play and creativity, post-postmodern leadership acknowledges complexity and fluidity in modern organizations. The importance of ethical leadership, flexibility, and distributed power structures was underscored, providing a balanced and pragmatic approach to managing contemporary organizational challenges.

The overview of post-postmodernism, metamodernism, and digimodernism established their origins and development, explaining the transition from modernism to postmodernism and beyond. Key thinkers and foundational texts were discussed, offering a deeper understanding of the core concepts. The significance of post-postmodernism in organizational theory lies in its ability to address the limitations of both modernism and postmodernism, offering a more balanced and constructive framework for understanding and managing modern organizations.

In the need for new leadership paradigms, we examined the shift from rigid hierarchies to flexible networks, the role of ethical leadership, and the importance of adaptive and distributed leadership. The integration of technology and cultural sensitivity were highlighted as essential components for effective leadership in a globalized business environment. These insights suggest a more nuanced, flexible, and ethically grounded approach to leadership that can adapt to the complexities of the modern business environment.

Emphasis on networks and relationships explored dynamic networks, interconnected actors, and the importance of trust and reciprocity. Case studies demonstrated the benefits of networked organizations, while strategies for fostering collaboration and communication were provided. Building and maintaining professional relationships through trust and reciprocity is essential for creating effective and innovative work environments.

Ethical considerations in leadership were examined, critiquing traditional ethical frameworks and introducing non-deontological approaches. Principles of metamodern ethics, such as flexibility, context-sensitivity, and responsiveness, were discussed. Case studies of ethical dilemmas and resolutions highlighted the importance of integrating ethics into organizational culture, demonstrating how ethical decision-making processes and models can be practically applied.

New forms of power and resistance addressed the shift from traditional power structures to more flexible and decentralized models. Understanding resistance in a post-postmodern context involves recognizing it as a valuable feedback mechanism. Strategies for managing and embracing resistance constructively were provided, emphasizing the importance of empowerment and inclusion. Case studies illustrated how organizations can successfully implement new power dynamics to foster innovation and employee engagement.

The integration of play and creativity highlighted the role of play in the workplace, providing historical context and benefits. Techniques for fostering creativity and innovation were discussed, along with practical strategies for promoting play at work. Measuring the impact of playful and creative initiatives is essential for understanding their effectiveness and justifying continued investment. Examples of creative organizational practices demonstrated how companies successfully integrate play and creativity into their cultures.

Hybrid approaches in organizational theory explored the rationale behind combining modern and postmodern elements. Case studies of hybrid organizational models provided insights into successful implementations, showing how these approaches balance stability and flexibility. Implementation strategies for integrating modern and postmodern principles were discussed, including tools and frameworks for hybrid organizational development. Balancing innovation and tradition is crucial for managing the tension between old and new paradigms, with examples of organizations successfully achieving this balance.

Global challenges and opportunities provided an overview of the global business environment, emphasizing the importance of cultural sensitivity and adaptation. Strategies for fostering cultural sensitivity were discussed, highlighting the role of cultural awareness in global business success. Case studies of successful global initiatives illustrated how organizations navigate and leverage global challenges and opportunities to drive growth and innovation.

The future of post-postmodern leadership was examined, emphasizing the dynamic, adaptive, and integrated nature of this leadership approach. Key themes included the importance of ethical leadership, networks and relationships, adaptive and distributed leadership, integration of technology, cultural sensitivity, and balancing innovation and tradition. Post-postmodern leaders are well-equipped to guide their organizations toward sustainable success in an ever-evolving global business landscape.

Future directions in post-postmodern organizational theory will likely focus on several emerging trends that further adapt and evolve the principles of leadership and management in the face of ongoing global changes. One significant trend is the increasing integration of advanced technologies such as artificial intelligence, machine learning, and big data analytics into organizational processes. These technologies will not only enhance decision-making and operational efficiency but also enable more personalized and adaptive management practices that can respond swiftly to changing market conditions and employee needs.

Another trend is the growing emphasis on sustainability and corporate social responsibility. Organizations will increasingly prioritize environmental stewardship and ethical practices, integrating these values into their core strategies. This shift reflects broader societal demands for businesses to contribute positively to the global community and address issues such as climate change, resource scarcity, and social inequality.

The rise of remote and hybrid work models is also transforming organizational structures and leadership approaches. Leaders will need to develop new skills and strategies to manage distributed teams effectively, fostering a sense of connection and collaboration despite physical distances. This trend necessitates a greater focus on digital communication tools, virtual team-building activities, and flexible work arrangements that accommodate diverse employee needs.

Cultural diversity and inclusion will continue to be paramount as organizations operate in increasingly globalized markets. Leaders will be tasked with creating inclusive environments that respect and leverage cultural differences, promoting equity and belonging within diverse workforces. This involves ongoing cultural competency training, inclusive policies, and practices that ensure all employees feel valued and supported.

The concept of agile leadership will become more prominent, with leaders adopting a mindset that embraces change and uncertainty. Agile leaders will prioritize continuous learning, adaptability, and resilience, encouraging their teams to innovate and experiment without fear of failure. This approach aligns with the post-

postmodern emphasis on flexibility and responsiveness, enabling organizations to thrive in dynamic and unpredictable environments.

Mental health and well-being will gain greater attention as essential components of organizational success. Companies will implement comprehensive wellness programs that address the physical, emotional, and psychological needs of their employees. This holistic approach to employee well-being will enhance productivity, reduce burnout, and foster a more engaged and motivated workforce.

Data-driven decision-making will play a crucial role in shaping future organizational strategies. Leaders will leverage data insights to understand market trends, customer preferences, and employee performance, making informed decisions that drive growth and innovation. This reliance on data will require robust analytics capabilities and a culture that values evidence-based practices.

The role of leadership will increasingly focus on purpose and meaning. Leaders will be expected to articulate a clear and compelling vision that aligns with the values and aspirations of their employees and stakeholders. By fostering a sense of purpose, leaders can inspire and motivate their teams, creating a shared commitment to achieving organizational goals.

Organizations will adopt more fluid and decentralized structures, moving away from rigid hierarchies. This shift will empower employees at all levels to take on leadership roles, contribute ideas, and drive initiatives. Decentralized structures promote agility, innovation, and a sense of ownership among employees, leading to a more dynamic and responsive organization.

The future of post-postmodern organizational theory will be shaped by trends such as advanced technology integration, sustainability, remote and hybrid work models, cultural diversity and inclusion, agile leadership, mental health and well-being, data-driven decision-making, purpose-driven leadership, and decentralized structures. These trends reflect the ongoing evolution of leadership and management practices, emphasizing adaptability, inclusivity, and responsiveness in a rapidly changing global business landscape.

As we conclude this exploration of post-postmodern leadership, it is imperative for current and future leaders to embrace and adapt the principles discussed to navigate the complexities of today's dynamic business environment. The world is evolving at an unprecedented pace, and traditional leadership models often fall short in addressing the multifaceted challenges organizations face today. By adopting post-postmodern principles, leaders can create resilient, innovative, and ethical organizations that thrive amidst uncertainty and change.

The first step is to acknowledge the necessity of integrating modern and postmodern elements. Leaders must appreciate the stability offered by traditional structures while embracing the flexibility and adaptability required for innovation. This balance is crucial for building organizations that can sustain long-term success while remaining agile enough to seize new opportunities and respond to emerging threats.

Emphasizing networks and relationships is central to post-postmodern leadership. Leaders should cultivate strong, collaborative connections within and outside their organizations, recognizing that these networks are the lifeblood of innovation and strategic execution. Building and maintaining trust, fostering open communication, and ensuring reciprocal relationships will enhance organizational cohesion and drive collective success.

Ethical leadership is no longer optional; it is a mandate. As stakeholders increasingly demand accountability and transparency, leaders must integrate ethical considerations into every decision. Developing a nuanced understanding of non-deontological ethics—flexibility, context-sensitivity, and responsiveness—will enable leaders to navigate complex moral landscapes and make decisions that are both principled and pragmatic.

Adaptive leadership is essential in a world characterized by rapid technological advancements and shifting geopolitical dynamics. Leaders should foster a culture of continuous learning and adaptability, encouraging their teams to embrace change and view it as an opportunity rather than a threat. This involves promoting a mindset that values experimentation, learning from failures, and iterating on successes.

The importance of distributed leadership cannot be overstated. Empowering employees at all levels to take initiative and contribute to decision-making processes fosters a sense of ownership and engagement. This decentralized approach not only leverages the collective intelligence of the organization but also enhances its ability to innovate and respond swiftly to market changes.

Leaders must also harness the power of technology to drive efficiency and innovation. By leveraging digital tools and data analytics, organizations can gain valuable insights, streamline operations, and enhance customer experiences. However, it is equally important to address the ethical and societal implications of technological advancements, ensuring that digital transformation aligns with broader organizational values and societal goals.

Cultural sensitivity and inclusivity are paramount in a globalized business environment. Leaders should prioritize creating inclusive environments that respect and leverage cultural differences, promoting equity and belonging within diverse workforces. This involves continuous cultural competency training, inclusive policies, and practices that ensure all employees feel valued and supported.

Balancing innovation and tradition requires clear vision and effective communication. Leaders must manage the tension between established practices and new approaches, integrating modern and postmodern principles to create a dynamic organizational culture. This balance enables organizations to maintain stability while fostering the agility needed to innovate and thrive in a rapidly changing landscape.

Adopting and adapting post-postmodern principles is not just a strategic choice; it is a necessity for leaders aiming to navigate the complexities of today's global business environment. By embracing these principles, leaders can build organizations that are not only resilient and innovative but also ethical and inclusive. The journey toward post-postmodern leadership is ongoing, requiring continuous learning, adaptation, and commitment. Let us move forward with confidence and determination, guided by the insights and strategies explored in this book, to create a future where organizations and their leaders can truly thrive.

Appendices

Practical Tools for Post-Postmodern Leadership

McKinsey 7S Model

Aligns structure, strategy, systems, shared values, skills, style, and staff to support hybrid approaches.

Agile Methodologies

Scrum and Kanban for iterative development, continuous feedback, and adaptive planning.

Design Thinking

Human-centered approach to innovation focusing on user needs, creative solutions, and iterative testing.

Collaborative Platforms

Tools like Microsoft Teams, Slack, and Trello for real-time communication and project management.

Balanced Scorecards

Framework for translating vision and strategy into specific, measurable objectives across multiple perspectives.

Lean Management Principles

Tools such as value stream mapping and continuous improvement cycles to maximize value and minimize waste.

Holacracy

Management framework that distributes decision-making authority across self-organizing teams.

Cultural Training Programs

Comprehensive programs to raise awareness and understanding of cultural differences among employees.

Employee Engagement Surveys

Regular surveys to measure job satisfaction, creativity, and engagement.

Innovation Metrics

Tracking new ideas generated, projects initiated, and successful innovations implemented.

Productivity and Performance Metrics

Comparing productivity levels and performance metrics before and after implementing new initiatives.

Feedback Mechanisms

Processes for gathering and acting on feedback from employees, customers, and other stakeholders.

Cross-Cultural Communication Tools

Training and platforms that facilitate clear and respectful communication across cultures.

Pilot Programs

Testing innovative ideas on a small scale before broader implementation.

Inclusive Leadership Training

Programs that equip leaders with skills for adaptive leadership, change management, and fostering innovation.

Remote Work Tools

Technologies and practices that support collaboration and productivity in distributed teams.

Wellness Programs

Comprehensive programs addressing physical, emotional, and psychological needs of employees.

Data Analytics Tools

Platforms for leveraging data insights to understand market trends, customer preferences, and employee performance.

Cultural Exchange Programs

Opportunities for employees to gain firsthand experience of different cultures.

Diversity and Inclusion Metrics

Measures to track progress and identify areas for improvement in cultural sensitivity and inclusivity.

Sustainability Frameworks

Guidelines and metrics for integrating environmental stewardship into business strategies.

Employee Resource Groups (ERGs)

Voluntary, employee-led groups that provide support and networking opportunities for diverse communities within the organization.

Adaptation of Business Practices

Modifying strategies, products, and management approaches to align with local cultural norms.

Ongoing Learning and Development Programs

Training sessions focused on continuous improvement and skill development for all employees.

Academic Resources

Vermeulen, N., & Van den Akker, R. (2010). Notes on Metamodernism. Journal of Aesthetics & Culture, 2(1).

This foundational paper explores the concept of metamodernism as an oscillation between modernist and postmodernist perspectives. It provides theoretical underpinnings for understanding how metamodernism can be applied to organizational theory, highlighting the blend of sincerity and irony, and the interplay of hope and doubt.

Lipovetsky, G., & Charles, S. (2005). Hypermodern Times. Polity Press.

Lipovetsky and Charles discuss the transition from postmodernism to hypermodernism, focusing on how accelerated consumerism and technological advancement impact society and organizations. This work provides insights into the pressures and opportunities for businesses operating in a hypermodern context.

Gergen, K. J. (1991). The Saturated Self: Dilemmas of Identity in Contemporary Life. Basic Books.

Gergen's exploration of postmodern identity offers valuable context for understanding the fluid and fragmented nature of organizational identities in a post-postmodern world. It is essential for comprehending how organizations can navigate and leverage these identities to foster innovation and adaptability.

Braidotti, R. (2013). The Posthuman. Polity Press.

Braidotti's work on posthumanism delves into the implications of postmodern theory for human identity and organizational behavior. This book provides a framework for understanding how organizations can adapt to the evolving nature of human-technology interactions and the ethical considerations involved.

Hassan, I. (1987). The Postmodern Turn: Essays in Postmodern Theory and Culture. Ohio State University Press.

Hassan's essays provide a comprehensive overview of postmodern theory and its cultural implications, offering a foundation for understanding the shift towards post-postmodernism. This resource is crucial for contextualizing the evolution of organizational theory.

Bauman, Z. (2000). Liquid Modernity. Polity Press.

Bauman's concept of "liquid modernity" explores the transient and flexible nature of contemporary life. This book is instrumental in understanding how organizations can navigate constant change and uncertainty, key themes in post-postmodern leadership.

Practical Resources

Kegan, R., & Lahey, L. L. (2009). Immunity to Change: How to Overcome It and Unlock the Potential in Yourself and Your Organization. Harvard Business Review Press.

This practical guide addresses the psychological and organizational barriers to change, providing tools and strategies for fostering adaptability and innovation in a post-postmodern context.

Brown, B. (2012). Daring Greatly: How the Courage to Be Vulnerable Transforms the Way We Live, Love, Parent, and Lead. Avery.

Brown's exploration of vulnerability and authenticity offers valuable insights for post-postmodern leaders seeking to build trust and resilience within their organizations. This book emphasizes the importance of empathy and open communication.

Scharmer, C. O. (2016). Theory U: Leading from the Future as It Emerges. Berrett-Koehler Publishers.

Scharmer's Theory U provides a framework for transformative leadership, emphasizing deep listening, co-creation, and leading from the future. This resource is essential for leaders looking to integrate post-postmodern principles into their organizational strategies.

Laloux, F. (2014). Reinventing Organizations: A Guide to Creating Organizations Inspired by the Next Stage of Human Consciousness. Nelson Parker.

Laloux explores the emergence of "teal organizations," which align closely with post-postmodern principles of distributed leadership, wholeness, and evolutionary purpose. This book provides case studies and practical guidance for implementing these concepts.

Gilmore, J. H., & Pine, B. J. (2007). Authenticity: What Consumers Really Want. Harvard Business Review Press.

Gilmore and Pine's work on authenticity in consumer behavior offers insights into how organizations can cultivate genuine relationships with their stakeholders. This book is particularly relevant for understanding the ethical and relational aspects of post-postmodern leadership.

Senge, P. M. (2006). The Fifth Discipline: The Art & Practice of The Learning Organization. Currency Doubleday.

Senge's seminal work on learning organizations provides tools and frameworks for fostering continuous improvement and adaptability. This resource is crucial for leaders aiming to cultivate a culture of innovation and learning in a post-postmodern environment.

These academic and practical resources provide a comprehensive foundation for understanding and implementing post-postmodern principles in organizational theory. They offer theoretical insights, practical tools, and case studies that leaders can use to navigate the complexities of the modern business landscape.

www.ingramcontent.com/pod-product-compliance
Lightning Source LLC
Chambersburg PA
CBHW071831210526
45479CB00001B/92